Steamers, Schooners, Cutters, and Sloops

Steamers, Schooners, Cutters, and Sloops

Marine Photographs of N.L. Stebbins
taken from 1884 to 1907

Selected and Annotated by
W.H. Bunting

Published for the
Society for the Preservation
of New England Antiquities
by Houghton Mifflin Co.,
Boston 1974

First Printing H

Copyright © 1974 by the Society for the Preservation of New England Antiquities

Printed in the United States of America

This project is supported by a grant from the National Endowment for the Arts, a federal agency, and contributions from the following individuals:

Mr. John Nicholas Brown
The Henry P. Kendall Foundation
Mrs. John J. Radley
Mr. Stephen B. Thayer

Design: Designs & Devices, Inc., Cambridge, Massachusetts

Text set in 9/11 pt. Caledonia Linofilm. Titles set in
24 pt. Franklin Gothic.

Library of Congress Cataloging in Publication Data

Bunting, William Henry, 1945–

   Steamers, schooners, cutters, and sloops.

   1. Photography of ships. 2. Steamboats. 3. Sailing ships. 4. Stebbins, Nathaniel Livermore, 1847–1922
 I. Stebbins, Nathaniel Livermore, 1847–1922 illus.
II. Title.
TR670.5.B86   779'.37'0924   74-12034
ISBN 0-395-19895-X

Dedication

It is a pleasure to dedicate this book to Miss E. Florence Addison, who has been an important friend to the Stebbins Collection. While serving as assistant to the director of the Society for the Preservation of New England Antiquities from 1920 until she retired in 1972, Miss Addison took a special interest in the welfare of the Stebbins material. Her concern for the careful preservation of the photographs was matched by her desire to have the collection used and appreciated. Her generous and intelligent assistance was noted by all who had dealings with her; timid and apprehensive students who arrived before her desk soon felt that they were being accorded all the courtesy and consideration which an established scholar might expect. Individuals who explored the Stebbins Collection as long ago as the early 1940's still inquire for news of "Miss Addison of the Preservation Society."

Introduction

Nathaniel Livermore Stebbins was a Boston-based commercial photographer who specialized in marine work, in business from 1884 until 1922 when he died, at the age of seventy-five. His records list about 25,000 photographs taken during his career, of which roughly 60 percent appear to have been of marine subjects. The majority of these marine photos concerned yachting, although the number dealing with commercial vessels was considerable. The remaining portion reflected a wide range of professional photographic work, including such subjects as hotel boiler rooms, theater scenes, and studies of Colonel Higginson's hounds.

After Stebbins' death, the collection (then numbering about 20,000 plates) was bought by another photographer, Mr. Edward U. Gleason, who had been associated with Stebbins' business for some years. Presumably there was still enough demand for certain well-known Stebbins photographs for Gleason to consider the purchase worthwhile. In any event, Gleason died in 1928, leaving no more provision for the welfare of the collection than Stebbins had.

Gleason's estate acted to dispose of the material promptly, and quickly sold the greater portion of the negatives for old glass. Tradition has it that these plates were used for panes in greenhouses. About one hundred plates, mostly of commercial sailing vessels, were bought by Carroll R. Sawyer, of Manchester, N.H., and a comparable lot of steamship negatives was purchased by Elwen M. Eldredge, a collector from Brooklyn. (The first group was eventually integrated into the photo collection of the Peabody Museum of Salem, while the steamship plates are now in the collection of the Mariners Museum.) The largest group of plates and prints to be saved was purchased by the Society for the Preservation of New England Antiquities through the efforts of the Society's founder and corresponding secretary, William Sumner Appleton. The Society's collection of Stebbins material totals over 5000 different photographs (counting duplicate negatives and prints as one) and includes over 2500 glass plates. The prints which were acquired had been mounted in thirty-six photo albums.

In the 1920's historic preservation was not yet a widely felt cause. It is apparent that even marine historians, though no doubt very interested in relics from the more distant past, were unimpressed by the Stebbins material. Rare is the person who can see the real significance of his daily surroundings, and in the 1920's there were still enough yachts, side-wheelers, and coasting schooners (to say nothing of hotel boiler rooms) to satisfy the casual observer. Indeed there is no indication that Stebbins himself saw anything of unusual value in his life's work. The history of early commercial photography is filled with tales of the destruction of thousands upon thousands of irreplaceable glass negatives, and in most cases the disposal was authorized by the photographers' surviving family members. No doubt even the rare photographer who believed that his plates represented more than simply sentimental value would have hesitated to ask his family to keep them, considering the intolerable problems created by the storage of twenty or thirty thousand eight-by-ten-inch glass plates in the average household.

William Appleton, very fortunately, was the right man in the right place at the right time. He is today remembered as one of the outstanding pioneers of American architectural preservation. He founded the Society for the Preservation of New England Antiquities in 1910, at a time when American millionaires still felt culturally compelled to build castle-like homes and import furnishings from Europe. The Society served as Appleton's base of operations in a lifelong effort to prevent the destruction and neglect of architecturally important New England houses, and to educate New Englanders in their rich heritage of buildings and artifacts. Today, the Preservation Society owns nearly sixty major properties in five New England states, and is the largest regional preservation organization in the country. With its long experience in the field, the Society has assisted in many other local preservation efforts.

While Appleton was primarily concerned with saving old houses and their furnishings, he had many other interests as well. As a result, he bought at junk prices a staggering quantity and assortment of "New England antiquities," leaving to his successors the tasks of storage and debate over the appropriateness of the Society's diversity of collections. His assessment of future antiquarian value has proven remarkably shrewd, although the variety of the Society's important holdings, which include wallpaper samples and fire apparatus, chairs and children's mugs, carriages and Stebbins photographs, may upset the sense of order of the more fastidious museum specialist. Of course, if Appleton had been so burdened by mental neatness, the photographs in this selection and the many others they represent would not have been saved. Evidence that Appleton's taste in acquisitions may have reflected true prescience, and not simply the instincts of a pack rat, is found in a letter concerning a house in Somerville, written in 1921: "This would make an ideal period house for the display of mid-Victorian black walnut (furniture) but the present is probably fifty years too early for anything of that kind . . ."[1]

A brief look into the particulars of the Stebbins purchase demonstrates that Appleton was no wild spendthrift, and increases one's respect for his many accomplishments. It is worth noting that while angling for the Stebbins material he was also involved in negotiations with state and local officials over the fate of a house, and was trying to raise $180 to purchase forty volumes of Prang greeting cards. In February 1929 he wrote the society president describing the Stebbins prospect:

. . . The estate wants to clean this up promptly. I find the junk dealers give 2 c. apiece for 8 x 10 glass and the Eastman people give 2½ c. delivered in Rochester. Most people can't take the trouble to deliver in Rochester, and accordingly sell to the junk man. At 3 c. for 2500 negatives, the price is $75.00 and at $3.00 a volume for 36 volumes, the price is $108.00. The rest of the junk might be figured at $25 for a total of $208.00. Tom and I rather favor asking a number of Eastern Yacht Club members to come across with fives and tens and get what we can in this way . . .

Next, he wrote the lawyer who was handling the estate:

My Dear Mr. Haywood,
    I have recently been in the office on Bowdoin Square and have looked over very briefly the Stebbins photographic outfit and material there. I am led to believe that it would be very difficult to make sales of prints from these negatives, and accordingly am valuing them for but very little above their price as old glass. The photographic albums have value for us but are in very bad condition. Altogether, I am, however, able to make you an offer of $200 for the entire contents of the room. This includes all the negatives and the thirty-six volumes of photographs, and also cameras, lenses, and all the photographic material in the office. This offer I can leave open until Saturday at one o'clock only, and if you can't see your way to accepting it before that time shall have to withdraw it.

P.S. I mean of course Saturday, February 9th. By photographic material I mean everything of every kind in the room, omitting nothing.

Appleton's next letter, dated February 11, was addressed to a prominent and wealthy yachtsman who some years previously had used many Stebbins photographs in a book. He began by recounting his original estimate, and continued from there. . . . "This [sum] is undoubtedly too low, but nevertheless I went so far as to offer the estate $200 last week, and am informed today that the offer is rejected. I was sure it would be, but wanted to get a line on Mr. Haywood's point of view."

He then proceeded to arrive at a revised appraisal, which, depending on such variables as the possible value of the lenses, and so on, he placed at from $330 to $660. The message, of course, was that the yachtsman could still be assured of seeing his money well spent if he wished to help the Society make a new offer.

Sad to say, the yachtsman's enthusiasm was restrained. He wrote that he already owned all the Stebbins prints he wanted, but did allow that he might join in with others if the collection were to go to the Eastern Yacht Club.

Appleton then contacted a third party, who apparently had a good line to the yachtsman, and explained that although his first concern was simply to see the collection saved, he did wonder if the Eastern Yacht Club was really the best depository. Exactly what transpired after this point is left unclear in the Society files. What is very clear is a bill of sale, dated May 24, 1929, giving the Society title to "All negatives, prints, unsold photographs, photographic equipment, office fixtures" for a grand total of $182.

At the Society headquarters in Boston the thousands of glass plates have been fitted with new protective liners and envelopes, and stored in a specially-fitted negative room. The print albums were added to the Society library, where over the years they have been enjoyed by many. Stebbins photos from the SPNEA have illustrated articles and books too numerous to mention. As Appleton indicated in his letter to the lawyer, some of the volumes were in poor condition in 1929; by recent years many had simply fallen apart. Worse, experts judged that the prints were slowly being destroyed by acid from the pages they were mounted on, and by poorly-rinsed developing chemicals. In 1973 the Preservation Society was awarded a matching grant from the National Endowment for the Arts which permitted the demounting and scientific treatment of the prints. Money was also allocated for the compilation of a catalog of the prints. Copies of this catalog will eventually be deposited in appropriate libraries in other areas of the country, thereby making the resources of the Stebbins Collection more readily available.

Nathaniel Stebbins was born in Meadville, Pennsylvania, in 1847, and died in West Somerville, Massachusetts, in 1922. The most fruitful research on Stebbins was accomplished in 1950 by Miss E. Florence Addison, who was then the assistant to the director of the Society. Miss Addison located Stebbins' daughter, Mrs. Katherine Stevens, living in Middlebury, Vermont. In response to Miss Addison's inquiries, Mrs. Stevens wrote:

> Nathaniel L. Stebbins was the son of Reverend Rufus P. Stebbins, a prominent Unitarian clergyman and, for twelve years, president of Meadville Theological School, and of his wife, formerly Eliza Livermore of Cambridge. From boyhood he had a great love of the sea and of ships. As a young man he made a voyage to South America as passenger on a sailing vessel, and this increased his longing to be always in sight of the ocean. (His first business ventures were in quite another line.) It was in about 1882 that he became interested in photography. I was a small child, but I remember well his improvised darkroom in our bathroom and the portraits of us all that he experimented with. Very soon he was ready to give his whole time to photography, and since there were few specializing in marine pictures, it was natural that he saw that field as one which offered little competition, as well as an opportunity to be on the sea. He did do other sorts of photography, in the season when marine work was not active. Much of this was theatrical, some was for railroads, and so on.
>
> Father was a member of the Corinthian and Eastern Yacht Clubs in Marblehead and of one in Boston. In order to be in touch with yachtsmen and yachting events, he had for some years a sturdy forty-foot sloop. One year he had a yawl, and another season he chartered a steam yacht. For big races, where he had to maneuver quickly, he would charter a tug. So much of my childhood and youth was passed on the sea during the summer. Cameras in those days were large, heavy things, and a box of glass plates in their holders was heavier. He sometimes had a boy to help carry them to the wharf, but I can still see his rather small, spry figure balancing by the rail in the heaving bow of the boat, while he lifted the great camera to get his shot. Of course we held our breaths, for he couldn't swim a stroke.
>
> In order to produce the *Illustrated Coast Pilot* Father passed the examinations for a licensed coast pilot from Machias to some point south of New York. Many of the photographs in that book were secured when he went on the routine trips of the lighthouse tenders, by permission of the United States Lighthouse Board.

Stebbins took up photography in his mid-thirties, very shortly after the introduction of the dry plate made outdoor photography practical. He was one of many new photographers who, with perspectives unhindered by the formal tradition of the studio and the head-clamp, entered the profession at the time of this great breakthrough. The old wet plate, by contrast, was too slow to freeze motion, and had to be developed immediately. The advance represented by the dry plate was revolutionary, and greatly influenced people's views of themselves and their world. (It is instructive, for example, to notice the less stylized treatment of waves in later nineteenth-century marine paintings.)

Very little is known about the business arrangements or the incomes of early photographers in general, or of Stebbins in particular. It is not known whether Stebbins relied solely on income earned from his business; his yachts and club memberships certainly indicate that either he or his wife had some independent means, but that remains conjecture. Photography was an acceptable hobby practiced by many gentlemen, and it would not have been impossibly odd for a man from a good background to undertake it on a full-time basis, as, at worst, an amusing and harmless profession. Of course, the struggling itinerant photographer who set up a portrait tent with traveling carnivals to immortalize farm boys would not have enjoyed similar social acceptance. While it was one thing for a gentleman to enjoy a session at the reins of a spirited driving team, it was quite another to drive a coal wagon for wages.

This is not to say that Stebbins was less than successful or resourceful in his business. No doubt he earned a living at it, and he obviously enjoyed the work. He was probably very shrewd to concentrate on yachting photography, since the sport claimed many of the most successful and prominent citizens of Boston. These people owned houses and businesses in addition to yachts, and it is reasonable to suppose that much of Stebbins' winter employment was cultivated during the summer. He was selected to photograph interiors of many fine homes and yachts, and was obviously well regarded personally as well as professionally.

Like many leading photographers of the time, Stebbins sold prints of popular subjects — particularly naval vessels and America's Cup contenders — mounted on cards, to the general public. It was customary for this type of work to be farmed out to studios which specialized in the business, and sales were probably handled by regular photo distributors who operated nationally.[2] Stebbins' photo cards may still occasionally be found in antique or second-hand book stores.

Stebbins was unusually enterprising in regard to publishing photos in book form, reflecting, no doubt, his yacht-club social orientation. *American and English Yachts*, published in 1887 by Scribner's, was his first. This was a large-format and expensively-produced book obviously intended for the growing yachting market. It included a brief, interesting text by Edward Burgess, who was then the leading (and most over-worked) American yacht designer. That Burgess was willing to write the text speaks highly for Stebbins.

This was followed in 1889 by *Yacht Portraits of the Leading American Yachts*, published by Stebbins at Boston, another large-format production. In his introduction, Stebbins described the book as a reference work for yachtsmen, and apologized for photographs "showing the yachts under unfavorable circumstances, or being in themselves without artistic merit" but which were nevertheless judged necessary for the completeness of the work.

Both of these books reflected the widespread interest in the direction of yacht design during these years.

Mrs. Stevens' letter mentions that Stebbins did photographic work for railroads. It is not surprising that there is no record of these photographs ever having been in his own collection, since they would have been retained by the railroads. In the nineteenth century many railroads had very progressive managers who were quick to recognize that photography could be an important form of record-keeping. It is possible that this sort of work gave Stebbins the idea for the remarkable *Illustrated Coast Pilot*, which he published in 1891. This book was intended to assist mariners, and presented photographic illustrations of most of the principal landmarks and aids to navigation from New York to Eastport, Maine. A second edition was published in 1896, with the additional coverage of the Southern Atlantic and Gulf Coasts. The *Illustrated Coast Pilot* was a very ambitious and innovative demonstration of the practical applications of photography. It marked a step in the evolution of photography from its early limited status as a quasi-art form to the multifaceted medium that it is today.

In 1896 Stebbins also published *The Yachtsman's Album*, an inexpensively-produced collection of 240 small illustrations of yachts, with data. In 1912 he published *The New Navy of the United States*, in similar format, which featured an introduction attributed to the Admiral of the Navy, George Dewey.

Photographs by Stebbins were occasionally published in Sunday newspaper supplements, and appeared in many maritime-oriented advertisements. For example, the schedules of the Eastern Steamship Lines were for many years illustrated with Stebbins steamer portraits. In the early 1900's Stebbins photographs were featured regularly in *The Rudder* magazine. The March 1901 issue contains an article written and illustrated by Stebbins entitled "A Flying Trip to Some English Yacht Yards in 1899." At this time *The Rudder* was a very sprightly publication, and Stebbins' photographs added much to its style.

Willard B. Jackson of Marblehead and Henry G. Peabody of Boston were also active Boston-area yachting photographers during much of Stebbins' career. Jackson's work closely resembles Stebbins', and their photographs have occasionally been mistakenly credited to each other. The technical quality of much of Peabody's work was unsurpassed; his photographs have a polish and a sharpness of image that is remarkable. In 1889 Peabody took first prize in a marine photography exposition held in Boston, in which Stebbins must also have participated. In 1891 he published a lavish volume of yacht portraits entitled *Representative American Yachts*, which was in the style of Stebbins' earlier books. The individual plates were flawless period pieces, more "perfect" than many of Stebbins', although the range of subject matter was limited and the overall tone was without the refreshing sense of openness and integrity of Stebbins' work. There is no record of the relationships between these three men beyond the photographic indications that they occasionally worked from the same vessel. Peabody, incidentally, first worked as a railroad photographer, and is best known for his years spent as a leading American landscape photographer.

Stebbins was also a contemporary to the excellent New York marine photographers James Burton and C. E. Bolles. And of course there were many others as well, there and elsewhere, both amateur and professional. No one, however, appears to have amassed or to have been survived by a collection of the size, variety, and time-span as that produced by Stebbins. His record of commercial vessels is unique, and is of very considerable historical value (it is ironic that much of this was probably the photographer-for-hire work Stebbins considered mundane). Yacht photography was Stebbins' real passion, and his yachting photos display his most relaxed style of picture-taking. To a nineteenth-century photographer the billowing white and diaphanous sails of yachts were perhaps reminiscent of neoclassical visions of draped Greek goddesses; in any event, they were apparently deemed more artistically and socially meritorious subjects than the work-stained sails of commercial vessels.

The chief value of Stebbins' work is derived from its subject matter, and the photographs from his first twenty years or so are, in my judgment, much more important than most of those taken later. From the eighties into the early 1900's Stebbins was recording the image of sweeping technological and social change. Although America's deep-water fleet was greatly diminished, the nation's major ports and coastal waters had never seen more varied traffic as coastal, foreign-flag, and yachting activity flourished. These decades saw the general displacement of commercial sail, and the dramatic and impressive improvement of steam navigation. Photographs taken quite matter-of-factly tell the fascinating tale: a fruit brig and steel refrigerated banana steamers; clipper fishing schooners and steam beam trawlers; full-rigged ships and steam cargo liners; walking-beam side-wheelers and turbine-screw coastal liners. Perhaps the greatest contrast is provided by photos of the little passenger-carrying bark *Sarah* bound for the Azores, and of the great North Atlantic steam greyhounds. Stebbins' many naval photographs record the rapid, though belated, development of the American steel navy. His yachting photography began in the era of traditional local types, and ended with the scientifically-designed racing classes of the 1920's. The collection includes photos of every type of powered yacht, from the largest class of steamer to the smallest motor dory.

Photographs taken in the last years of Stebbins' career are generally of less variety, reflecting the consolidation of steam's dominance, the decline of locally-owned commercial shipping, and the standardization of yacht design. The adoption of the jib-headed mainsail, and the graduated income tax marked the end of the great era of yacht photography. It is probably only coincidental that the actual photographs from these final years were no doubt taken by associates, since Stebbins was by then quite elderly. Marine photography, in particular, required physical strength and good balance, and Stebbins — despite the wonderfully sturdy sound of his name — was of light build, and appears almost frail in a photograph taken late in life.

Nathaniel Stebbins died in his West Somerville home on July 10, 1922. His death passed without comment in the Boston papers, or, more surprisingly, in *Yachting*, or in *The Rudder*, which had benefited so much from his work. Had he died twenty years sooner, he probably would have rated a few words somewhere, but by the twenties photography no longer had an aura of novelty or magic, a commercial photographer was just another tradesman, and maritime interest was in decline.

Any fair assessment of Stebbins' work must include at least a glance at the record of the great treasure of plates which were destroyed and of which the Society has no prints. Browsing in Stebbins' negative books is a truly depressing activity:

New York pilot comes aboard. Party on [barkentine] *Rachel Emery*. McKee Lighter Co. putting boiler into ferry boat. Group on [full-rigged] ship *Independence*. *Sooloo*, [full-rigged] ship at wharf. *Right Arm* [tug] and wrecked barque *Culdoon*. *Bruce Hawkins*, [barkentine], disabled. Walter Baker & Co. teams. Engine room, steamer *Yorktown*. Turbine windmill. Deck & forecastle, barque *Freeman*. Whitney Steam Carriage grade trial. Steerage passengers on [Cunarder] *Pavonia*. Brig *Rapid Transit* at wharf.

Undoubtedly prints of many lost plates still exist, stored away in homes and businesses. I well remember finding one while visiting a delightful eighty-six-year-old former railroad man, who lived in a cottage stuck off in the woods of western Massachusetts. Housekeeping was not the old gandy dancer's forte, and the overstuffed chairs were slick with grime and upholstered in dog hair. The atmosphere was rich with the combined aromas of kerosene fumes, five elderly and over-fed dogs, a one-legged crow, and twenty years of cigar smoke, all a-simmer from the heat of two stoves running wide open, with throttles "in the corner." While the old man swayed about the room like a drunken belly dancer, demonstrating how he balanced on shaking bridge trusses while heavy freight trains rolled beneath him, my eyes were fixed by a wonderful "lost" Stebbins framed on the wall. It was taken in 1886, and showed the grounded remains of the tug *John Markee*, a victim of a boiler explosion. A man and a boy sat on the rail cap, while two boys in a dory hung on to the rudder. Beyond, a coasting schooner and a lighter lay at an East Boston lumber shipper's wharf.

The librarian of the Preservation Society would appreciate hearing from anyone who may own "lost" Stebbins prints. Although there are not, at present, sufficient funds available for purchase of copy negatives or prints, the information will be filed for possible future reference. Of course, any contributions of Stebbins material would be very gratefully received, in the interest of making the collection as complete as possible.

The selection of a relative handful of photographs from several thousand was necessarily a very frustrating and, in the end, a very arbitrary business. While some of the chosen photographs would probably have made anyone's collection, others were blessed simply because they chanced to be lying before me during a rare fit of decisiveness. These are all good, worthwhile photographs, but they are only representative of many others which could have as readily been used.

The selection was made with two basic constraints. First, it was decided that more than half of the photographs should be of yachting subjects, since they form a majority of the collection and reflect Stebbins' prime interest. Also, relatively little of Stebbins' yachting work has been published within the past forty years.

Second, no photographs were used which appear in the book *Portrait of a Port: Boston, 1852–1914*, by W. H. Bunting, published in 1971 by the Harvard University Press. *Portrait of a Port* contains over ninety Stebbins photographs, mostly of commercial vessels, and mostly from the Preservation Society collection. The selections in *Steamers, Schooners, Cutters, and Sloops* and *Portrait of a Port* are thus complementary, and together form a fair retrospective of the work of a notable early American photographer. The photographs amply demonstrate our debt to Stebbins and to William Sumner Appleton, for these men have provided us with informative and wonderfully entertaining images from a very interesting and different age.

The captions are intended — except in the case of the steamer *General Slocum* portrait — to enhance the reader's enjoyment of the photographs. All the references indicated by the notes come recommended by this annotator, who relied heavily upon them, and who is thankful for the efforts of the authors cited.

The idea for this book originated within the SPNEA. The dogged efforts of Daniel Lohnes and Stanley Smith ensured the project's completion, and I thank them. I wish also to thank the several friends who cast sharp eyes over the manuscript. David Cheever, Jr., who is a small boat yachtsmen in the finest old-time Buzzards Bay tradition, deserves special mention for his many contributions and valued encouragement.

The photographs are not presented in any particular order, and some have been cropped.

The only person I know who remembers having met Nathaniel Stebbins in person is John Leavitt, the marine artist and historian. John remembers entering the photo studio on Bowdoin Square with his father in about 1921, when he was a young boy. He recalls being introduced to a small, kindly old man who was puttering happily about, surrounded by mountains of dark glass plates.

Steamers, Schooners, Cutters, and Sloops

The sandbagger *Hurley* on the Delaware River

The sandbagger *Hurley* racing on the Delaware. The burgee of the Quaker City Yacht Club flies from her peak. It would appear that she might be doing better with her jib set, but no doubt her skipper knows his business better than we do; judging from the sandbagger ahead, the wind is puffy. Beyond the weekend flyers a deeply-laden coastal schooner comes soberly along, working for her keep.

Many of the most interesting Stebbins photographs date from the mid-eighties, the first years of his career. It is a very great pity that a disproportionate number of prints and plates from this period are missing. His albums from these years are few in number, and contain a sparse and seemingly random selection of prints, while the sequential numbers on the small lot of surviving negatives jump by the hundreds from plate to plate.

The sandbaggers — so-called because they carried shifting ballast in the form of sandbags — were the reigning type of American racing craft from the fifties well into the eighties. Francis Herreshoff judged in 1958 that the sandbaggers probably "had the fastest average speed for their length overall of any type of boat that has been accepted as a type."[3] They ranged in length from about eighteen feet to almost thirty feet and typically were skillfully constructed with great lightness. They were fit only for sheltered waters, and had to be judiciously managed in a breeze, particularly if the crew had guessed wrong and left their sandbags ashore. If the wind dropped during a race the sand was simply dumped overboard.

Sandbaggers were developed from indigenous shoal-draft working vessel types, and it is interesting that although geographically widespread, they were fundamentally similar. While sandbaggers were built and raced at Boston, Philadelphia, Charleston, Savannah, New Orleans, and places in between, the greatest centers of activity were New York Harbor and the western reaches of Long Island Sound. In the sixties sandbagger racing caught the attention of wealthy sportsmen, and many yachts were owned in the manner of race horses. Others were owned by working men, watermen, or even by sporting taverns; sandbagger racing was vigorously free from class or social restrictions, and aroused intense public interest. The crews were all professionals to the extent that they at least shared in the winnings, and were often composed of watermen. Racing was for cash stakes, and the New York area championships in the seventies were sailed with $1000 up per boat, and as much as $50,000 in side bets.

It was rough sport, and anything was fair if you could get away with it. A crew that lost a race could often seek satisfaction in a fight afterwards. Cary Smith, the marine designer and artist, started out in sandbaggers, and recalled that for long Sunday races food and liquor were carried in a special locker which customarily could not be opened until the first mark had been rounded. Pie was always on the menu, and it was served on rugged Welsh iron pie plates. If the race turned into a drifter and lasted after twilight, six or eight pie plates worked skillfully and silently as paddles over the lee side could very much improve the sandbagger's position.[4]

Sandbag racing was destroyed by the measurement reforms of the eighties, which outlawed shifting ballast in order to encourage a healthier breed of yacht, and by the growing "Corinthian" or amateur yachting movement. The desirability of shifting the emphasis away from the sandbagger type of yacht cannot be questioned; the Corinthian movement, however, in this instance may not have been so charitably motivated. The development of yacht types which were less labor intensive and did not require large, combative weekend crews made yacht racing a more economically and socially exclusive sport. The Larchmont Yacht Club, an old sandbag club, may have been recognizing this loss when in later years it sponsored annual races for Long Island Sound oyster sloops.

It is with tears in the eye that the genuine old sandbagger recalls his glory — the days of the *Susie S.*, *Pluck and Luck*, *Zoe*, *Dare Devil* and *Mary Emma* — the days when twenty-seven footers went to windward under a rig that measured on the foot, from tip of horn to end of boom, seventy feet. Ah boys! despite all they say, there was a big chunk of fun knocked off this side of the world when we laid the old bag-wagons ashore and left them to rot . . . In the eyes of the racing yachtsman of '92 the carrying of a large crew is a felony, and shifting ballast *lese majeste*. "A racing machine, sir; dangerous, extremely dangerous!" . . . Seven or eight hundred good dollars would buy a man something in the sand-bag line, but what can you get for that money in these days of fin-keels and silk headed sails?[5]

Stebbins copy negative 933

On the Delaware sandbaggers were apparently raced through the eighties (shifting ballast seems to have been permitted by a few New York area clubs into the nineties). C. P. Kunhardt wrote that the Delaware sandbagger *Cahill,* characteristic of her type and, typically, named for her owner, was seventeen feet, six inches on deck; she was actually longer on the waterline, since the racing measurement was based solely on the "overall length" and did not include her ram bow and reverse-raked transom. Her thirty-two-foot mast was stayed from protruding boomkins similar to the arrangement shown on the *Hurley.* Her boom was twenty-seven feet long, her gaff sixteen feet, and she carried ninety-five yards of sail. The centerboard was fitted well aft, where, with a large skeg and a barn-door rudder, it attempted to balance the big mainsail. She normally carried a crew of eight.

> The racing catboats of the Delaware River differ from those of New York waters in being finer in the after end and sharper in the floor . . . Boats of this class are of course sailed with shifting ballast, and a numerous crew who lay out to windward by holding on to lines with toggles in the end. One man at the helm, another at the sheet, and a third at the peak [halyard] are required in a breeze to keep the boat from capsizing. A racing boat may be said to be constantly more or less on the verge of capsizing, and nothing but the incessant vigilance and dexterity of the crew will save her from going over. In the case of an upset, a frequent occurrence, the sandbags slip off and the crew crawl over and cling to the bottom until rescued by the help which is usually at hand on a crowded river.[6]

The *Hurley* appears to have fourteen or fifteen men aboard, and many of them look to be black. If so, they are probably regular Delaware River watermen.

Stebbins copy negative 933 (detail)

The full-rigged ship *Hotspur*

The ship *Hotspur*, of New Bedford, puts to sea from Boston on her maiden voyage. She is bound for Melbourne under charter to Peabody's line of "Australasian packets," and is undoubtedly carrying a cargo of general manufactured merchandise.

The *Hotspur* was owned principally in New Bedford and Boston, and was built on the Kennebec at Bath, Maine, the most important wooden shipbuilding center in the final decades of sail. Although comparatively small, she was otherwise a handsome example of the latter-day "Down Easter" type of square-rigged merchantman. Her hull has a healthy freeboard and a pleasing sheer with nicely balanced ends. Aloft she is very well sparred, with three skysail yards, and spencers on fore and main.

The black stack from the forward house shows that she is fitted with a steam donkey engine. Steam hoisting engines became increasingly popular in the last Down Easters, reflecting the increasing expense and difficulty of manning a deep-water sailing vessel properly. The engine, along with all the other important furniture of the vessel, was manufactured at Bath, which possessed a remarkably complete shipbuilding establishment.

Sailors on each mast are casting off the gaskets and overhauling the gear as the new canvas is set to the breeze. The fore royal braces have been slacked just preparatory to hoisting the yard.

As a group, the Down Easters spent most of their prime years in the California-to-Europe grain trade or in long distance trades to the Far East. Because their masters spent so much time at sea, often accompanied by their families, these men insisted on unusually fine accommodations in the cabin. Since they were also customarily part owners in the new vessel, they had influence in these matters. The cabins of the *Hotspur* (two passenger staterooms were fitted in the forward cabin) were finished in rosewood, bird's-eye maple, cherry, ash, and black walnut. The joinery was doubtless all that could be desired.[7]

After the Civil War, America's fleet of deep-water square-riggers declined steadily before a combination of social and economic pressures. By 1885 the construction of square-riggers was all but finished, as shipping profits were constricted between rising costs and increased competition from foreign steamships and metal-hulled sailing vessels. Morale aboard many Down Easters was very low, caused in part by the harsh discipline of American mates. To the very end, however, the standards of seamanship and the quality of the vessels remained high.

In a sense the Down Easters were fortunate to expire as they did, without being perverted through a protracted struggle for survival by means of unfortunate economies of design. Usually it seems to be the final vessels of a type that are the longest remembered. The last wall-sided steel European sailing carriers and the cavernous multi-masted American schooners are today popularly recognized to the exclusion of vast numbers of more representative and conceivably more admirable smaller vessels which preceded them. The wooden Down Easter, with but a few exceptions, was not subjected to an awkward period of unnatural enlargement. The Down Easters we remember probably represented the finest development of the wooden ocean carrier.

The *Hotspur*, however, would hardly be remembered at all had not several of Stebbins' fine portraits of her survived. She will thus always be considered in the crispness of her youth, for in 1887 she was lost on a coral reef while bound with a cargo of coal from New South Wales for Manila.

The surviving Stebbins photographs do not include very many deep-water sailing vessels, although several of the Down Easter portraits, in particular, are among the very best surviving studies of these vessels under sail. Most were taken at the outset of maiden voyages from Boston, and necessarily date from the first two years of Stebbins' professional career. They were obviously taken on order; Stebbins apparently had no great interest in the vessels as such, and rarely photographed them in port, although many tall masts appear in the backgrounds of his photos of tugs, ferries, and other harbor craft.

Stebbins copy negative 715

Regatta in Boston Harbor

July 4, 1885

A portion of the "third class keel sloops" racing in the City Regatta held off City Point. The sloop in the foreground is the *Nydia*; the *Alice* and the dark *Wildwave* are to the right. As usual, the overall winner was the "second class centerboard sloop" *Shadow*. Nearly eighty yachts participated in the affair, and the *Globe* reported:

> N. L. Stebbins took a large number of views from the [committee tug] *William H. Clark*.

The *Transcript* reported:

> It was comparatively quiet in Boston last Saturday, for a holiday. Of course, there were immense throngs of people in the streets and on the Common, and the small boy made noise enough with his horn, torpedoes and fire-crackers, but there were fewer fires to alarm folk, fewer accidents, and no appalling disasters.

Not that the day was without serious note. Thomas Riley received $50 for winning the mile swim in the Charles. Thousands of spectators cheered on the winner of the single sculls, who collected $250 for his efforts. Rowing events were also held on Jamaica Pond. Field sports were held in South Boston, where J. T. Maxwell won a first prize by throwing a fifty-six-pound weight twenty-six feet, four and one half inches. There were bicycle races, of course, and hurling on the Common. A local pick-up lacrosse team met the Canadian world champions, and the *Transcript* was kindly in its coverage: ". . . the Boston players made a plucky fight and showed that if they had had more practices together the Canadians would have been obliged to play with more care and spirit in order to be sure of a victory."

The Declaration of Independence was read at the official ceremonies, presided over by the mayor, who was an Irishman. The traditional Boston Oration was delivered by yet another Irishman, who was obviously aware of the significance of the moment. While he could not resist taking a few cuts at the Yankee establishment, his general statement was optimistic and friendly, and was at least not overladen with the empty patriotic mouthings so common to such an occasion. However, a few dusty feathers may have been ruffled by his evaluation of the role of Irishmen in the winning of the Revolution.

A great crowd gathered for the ascension of Dr. Allen and his balloon from the Common. The "doctor" first descended into Saugus Center, but rose once again and blew on to Wakefield. At night the city was treated to a large fireworks display.

Celebrations in outlying towns were similar. Fully ten thousand persons gathered at Walden Pond in Concord for a reform meeting. Speakers discussed patriotism, the advancement of the colored race, women's suffrage, and alcoholism.

Sweeping judgments as to the relative goodness or badness of life in past times must always be treated with the utmost suspicion. Nevertheless, it is tempting to cite the foregoing description as evidence supporting the impression that the period of the eighties was a particularly energetic and engaging moment in American history, especially in the Northeast. The manner in which a people celebrate their holidays can indeed be revealing.

Today we celebrate the Fourth very differently. A midweek Fourth, in particular, perplexes us and may almost be considered a public nuisance, since we no longer know how to celebrate at home. The automobile is not the only villain; consider too, the gray and dismal grouches who have deprived American boys of their fireworks, and, by extension, at least half the fun of boyhood. Adults who never thrilled to the aroma of punk and exploded two-inchers as children can never have real passion for the Fourth.

My axe being now well-ground, we may return to the historic facts. In the eighties the average Glorious Fourth resulted in many fires and gory casualties. A *Transcript* editorial writer, with some reluctance, called for the restriction of firecrackers from the city proper, not so much to preserve the fingers and eyes of the slow-witted, as to reduce the injuries and turmoil resulting from the lobbing of explosives under horses. Females apparently suffered more tragically than males from serious burns, no doubt on account of their long, flammable skirts. The many patriotic citizens who managed to shoot themselves and their neighbors, or who fell in the paths of locomotives, indicates that intoxication was then — as it remains today — a major cause of holiday death and injury.

Stebbins copy negative 548

The sloop *Shadow*

The celebrated sloop *Shadow* ghosts along in Boston Harbor with a cutter-style club topsail aloft, and a bonnet laced beneath her spinnaker, alow. For many years the *Shadow* was the most successful and famous American yacht. She was long thought to represent "the perfection of racing speed possible on thirty-four L.W.L."[8] Built in 1872, she was practically unbeatable for fifteen years, and in later years remained a serious threat. She burned in 1908 while laid up for the winter.

The *Shadow*'s finest day came in 1881 when she defeated the barnstorming Scotch cutter *Madge*, despite being five feet shorter. Until meeting the *Shadow*, the crack *Madge* had been enjoying an unblemished American career, sowing confusion in the hearts of all true Americans who swore by the obvious superiority of the centerboard yacht.

The *Shadow*, in fact, was no brainless skimming dish. She was built from a study model cut by Nat Herreshoff, then fresh out of MIT and employed in the pattern shop of the Corliss Engine Works. She was designed in the tradition of Narragansett Bay catboats, and combined a centerboard and fourteen foot beam with deep, full garboards and five feet, four inches draft, with the board up. As Herreshoff recalled:

> My idea at the time was to shape the hull so the ballast would be lower, have the bilges practically out of the water so as to get easy lines when the vessel is upright, and great beam that would give stability when keeled in a breeze . . . At that time the mention of placing ballast outside the hull was frowned upon, as it would surely make a vessel logy, and cause loss of rig if rough water were encountered.[9]

According to Herreshoff, the *Shadow* was the first "compromise" model yacht, although the term is more usually first applied to the later Burgess sloops. His claim is supported by Professor George Owen's belief that the *Shadow* was probably non-capsizable.[10] When first brought out she was fitted while racing with a mechanical ballast shifting device mounted athwartship in the cabin.[11]

Although at least several boats were built with the specific intention of beating the *Shadow*, her model does not appear to have been copied or improved upon for many years.[12] This is probably an indication of the tenacity with which traditional local notions of small boat form were held. In the seventies and early eighties the business of small boat design was still firmly in the realm of art and habit rather than science. In most areas the design was the work of the builders, and builders, by nature, were a conservative and suspicious lot.

The American preference for beamy, shoal yachts slowed growth of the science of yacht design, since whenever there arose a question about a prospective model's stability it was a simple matter just to build her a little wider. There was thus no incentive for the designer to learn mathematical computations. The use of shifting ballast into the early eighties was involved with the preference for beamy models in a sort of chicken-and-egg relationship. Ballast so carried exerted leverage as a function of its distance from the centerline, and of the angle of heel.[13]

Stebbins copy negative 1454

The barkentine *Rachel Emery*

Late summer 1884

The Boston barkentine *Rachel Emery*, bound out for the River Plate, with a deckload of New Hampshire pine. Temporary pinrails are fastened to her foremast shrouds. Sail has just been set, and there are heavy halyards to be coiled, and many buntlines and clewlines to be set to rights. A bight of the foresheet drags overside, and one cannot help thinking that if Stebbins were really on top of the situation he would have called it to the attention of the mate before taking the photograph, for surely that dragging line could ruin the picture for a touchy perfectionist of an owner or master. The dark pall of smoke from the tug would also probably not be appreciated. These are typical of details which are easily overlooked at the time, but which can be very distracting on the final prints. It is perhaps indicative that the photo was taken during Stebbins' first season in the business.

Nothing can obscure the fact that the *Emery* was a fine-looking specimen of a barkentine, and that she is being matter-of-factly put to sea by men who know their business. In the accepted fashion of a square-rigger, her yards are braced progressively squarer, from foreyard to royal, while in proper schooner manner the big spanker is sheeted well out. The woman and two children on the after cabin are probably members of the captain's family, and although they may be making the voyage, it is more likely that they will shortly be returning to Boston with the tug.

When hired to record the departure of a Boston sailing vessel on a deep-water voyage, Stebbins usually made a half-dozen or so exposures, and his records show that he usually took at least one formal photograph aboard of the "party, aft." It was customary for some of the owners, family and friends, to tow down to sea, especially if the vessel were new like the *Emery*. Such a group portrait was taken aboard the *Emery* and is listed in Stebbins' notebook, but has not survived.

John S. Emery Company was a well-established Boston shipping firm involved in trades with the Caribbean, South America, and Africa. Barkentines were nicely suited to this business. The rig held a particularly symbolic position in the great trade to the River Plate, which attracted a very large number of "coasting" schooners in addition to the regular deep-water square-riggers.[14]

Trade between New England and "the River" was of long standing, but it reached its most active state during the eighties, when a great influx of European investment and emigration to the Argentine created an unprecedented demand for lumber and manufactured items. Boston and Portland became the centers of New England's trade to "the River."

The return cargoes of hides, wool, or Caribbean sugar were the raw materials for New England's textile, shoe, and sugar refining industries. The effects of the successive boom and bust of the Argentine economy in the late eighties and early nineties directly influenced the prosperity of New England's shipbuilders and schooner owners.[15]

The crew aboard the *Rachel Emery* are looking forward to a generally leisurely passage (barring the possibility of meeting a tropical hurricane at this season) of from forty to eighty days' duration. The route taken by sailing vessels was 7500 to 8000 miles in distance, and extended through the frustrating latitudes of the equatorial doldrums. The vessels for the River usually sailed in the late summer or early fall, when the timber cut the previous winter had been sawn and delivered to the wharves.[16] Schooners, in particular, were thus spared a rugged winter on the coast, although no doubt many a New England sailor slapping mosquitoes on a sweltering night up a tributary river, where his vessel was slowly being loaded with beef bones, must have nearly been driven to dream longingly of the pleasures of a northwest gale in February.

Perhaps the most widespread misconception concerning the history of the age of sail involves the apparently high incidence of vessel losses. This is not surprising, since shipwrecks were always noteworthy, and any sailing vessel operated long enough was likely to come to grief eventually. The frequent founderings of vessels that were old and strained beyond seaworthiness is testimony to the fact that these vessels had sailed successfully for enough years to achieve a state of structural deterioration. Meaningful data as to the actual efficiency of sailing vessels in various trades is difficult to discover. The figures which Captain W. J. L. Parker has recently compiled concerning the activity of schooners in the trade to the River are thus especially fascinating. Of the 262 sailings of American schooners which he considered, only two vessels were lost through stress of weather.[17] One of these casualties was a big four-master, dismasted in a December gale shortly after sailing. This schooner fell victim to being too young rather than too old, for she was brand-new and lost her rig from the too rapid stretching of her new standing rigging.

Stebbins copy negative 426

The schooner yacht *Dauntless*

March 12, 1887

The schooner yacht *Dauntless* departs New York's Lower Bay, bound for Queenstown, Ireland, in a match race across the wild and wintry North Atlantic. Her rival, the new schooner *Coronet*, has already run past photographer Stebbins.

The little American bark astern of the *Dauntless* is under tow, her tug hidden behind the schooner's sails. The "Marine Intelligence" columns for the day list departures by several American barks; the larger *Belle of Oregon* was bound out for India; this little hooker is perhaps the *Atlantic*, of New Haven, for Bridgetown, Barbados. The brisk northerly wind will give her a fair chance for an offing from the coast, although "flying light," in ballast, she may soon be doing some wonderful rolling.

Although the *Dauntless* is carrying every imaginable sail, including a "pigeon wing topsail" over her square yard, her big regulation schooner-mainsail appears to be doing most of the work. Her lower masts were cut down by five feet in expectation of a lively passage; the forty-six-foot topmasts were left at full length with the expectation that they would be housed whenever conditions warranted. The sixteen sailors shipped forward on the yacht are probably sociologically indistinguishable from the crew signed aboard the little white bark astern, being, no doubt, northern Europeans with a majority of Scandinavians. Captain Crosby of the *Coronet* was greatly amused by the fuss that was made over his smart "American" crew at Cowes when, in fact, there was not an "American" among them.[18]

The master of the *Dauntless* for the race was none other than Captain Samuel "Bully" Samuels, who had made a name for himself driving men and ships in the bad old days of the North Atlantic sail packet trade. The *Dauntless* could only hope to beat the bigger *Coronet* if she were driven harder, and the sixty-four-year-old Samuels came out of retirement for the job. (A victory would not have hurt the sales of his thrilling "autobiography," published that year.) In 1866 Samuels had sailed the schooner yacht *Henrietta* to victory over the schooners *Vesta* and *Fleetwing* in the famous December race from New York to Cowes. The *Henrietta's* time was thirteen days, twenty-two hours.

The *Dauntless* was also an old-timer, having been built in 1866 and rebuilt in 1869. She had made numerous transatlantic passages and had been sailed hard under several owners, and it is not surprising that she leaked badly in the race. The terrible punishment she endured under the relentless will of Bully Samuels is proof of her excellent construction. One black night found the old vessel scudding at great speed under bare poles before hurricane-force winds. Twenty-eight-degree water indicated that there were icebergs in the neighborhood, but the old man's nerve was colder yet. Her run for the day (by dead reckoning) was 326 miles, and the main chainplates were started.[19] Winter racing on the North Atlantic demanded the most skilled application of the most imprudent seamanship.

The *Coronet* experienced similar conditions. With the wind near one hundred miles an hour and icebergs expected, Captain Crosby elected to heave to, which was no simple feat in itself. Once around, the schooner spent a relatively comfortable night with Atlantic combers breaking on deck. A guest described the scene below: "Captain, officers, guests, cook, steward, cabin-boy lay around in one confused mass, stowed away in the bunt of the squaresail or under the mess-table and stealthily improvising everything within reach to keep dry."[20]

Bully Samuels' single-minded excesses were all in vain, for the powerful *Coronet* sailed to an easy victory in fourteen days, nineteen hours. The *Dauntless* finished thirty hours later.

It should be mentioned that the *Dauntless*'s owner, Caldwell Colt, participated in the race. While most sportsmen would have felt that exposure to such great danger and discomfort was soley the business of paid crews, Colt, who had inherited a fortune from firearms, went just for the grand experience of it all. It was well that he did, for after the ship's water tank ruptured (according to another version, it had never been filled) all hands had to subsist on potables from the cabin stores. It is not recorded whether these life-preserving beverages were served in the famous round-bottom tumblers with which the *Dauntless*'s pantry was equipped.

Stebbins plate 1241

The Boston Harbor tug *Fannie Lenox*

The tug *Fannie Lenox* steams home to Boston late in the day. A weather vane intended for a barn graces her pilot house; the whistle looks a casualty from an epic temper-tantrum. Deckhands, like many workers, commonly wore waistcoats; in the nineteenth century everyone wore a hat.

The *Lenox* appears to be of the better class of small tug, since she apparently possesses a condensing engine; tugs with non-condensing engines could be recognized under way by the plume of steam they wore. A condenser added power and efficiency by creating vacuum in the cylinders, while the ability to recirculate boiler water vastly increased the tug's steaming range.

> The cost of a new tug varies from $8,000 to $70,000. There may be a few cheaper than $8,000, but they are the "poor white trash" of the tug family. The eight-thousand-dollar tug is built of wood and is generally from fifty to eighty feet long, engined with plain high-pressure non-condensing machinery and manned by three, four, or five men — a pilot, an engineer, and one or two deck hands. Many of these little fellows are known as "tramps" — that is, they loaf about the outer harbor seeking what they may devour in the way of an odd job ... With careful attention and considerate grooming they live to the ripe old age of five or six years. When they die nobody is the wiser, for the disappearance of one little tramp in the great army of tugs is like the blowing away of a cloud fleck in the sky.
>
> *New York Times*, May 4, 1891

The nineteenth century was the Age of the Tool. This inevitably progressed and merged into the great Age of the Misuse of the Tool, which we are presently trying to survive. The most striking difference between the nineteenth century and all the previous history of man is that for the first time people were contriving tools which allowed them to profoundly increase the scale of human activity. And tools begat still more tools.

The *Fannie Lenox* was a nineteenth-century tool; more importantly, she was a transportation tool. Transportation was central to the story of the nineteenth century, and is the foundation of American history. Compared to tools of today she is a crude affair of innocent simplicity, but in her day she served very well indeed. She is characteristic of the best of nineteenth-century tools in that she is a blend of functional requirements with a gifted artisan's sure sense of proportion and style. She communicates a spirit of logical, practical optimism which, however misplaced or misapplied, makes her a joy to contemplate.

By contrast, many modern vessels — witness the average bulk carrier or container ship — were apparently designed by computers and built by robots, and have all the style of a financial statement. Fortunately, there are some exceptions, and among them I would include the spare but distinctly stylish big tugs which now push huge coastal oil barges into Boston. They are worthy successors to the big sea-going coastal tugs (the $70,000 tugs mentioned in the article) which towed coal barges to New England in Stebbins' day.

There are a number of fine tug photos in the Stebbins Collection, including both harbor and coastal vessels. Many of the tugs were photographed from a pier head, presumably thus qualifying for a cheaper rate. The portrait of the *Fannie Lenox* has a very different feel from the usual obviously posed and commissioned tug photos, and I suspect it may be a rare spontaneous study of a commercial craft. If I seem a little irked with Stebbins over this matter, it is because the relative handful of such (surviving) photographs is so very outstanding, and it is a great pity that he didn't take more.

Stebbins copy negative 5727

The sloop *Minerva* on the Delaware River

A fascinating glimpse of yachting on the Delaware as the sloop *Minerva* sweeps past the well-populated little sloop serving as stakeboat.

The *Minerva* was built at Camden, New Jersey, in 1877, by one J. Collins. Research would probably show that Mr. Collins was primarily a producer of oyster sloops, which the *Minerva* strongly resembles. Her big, single headsail is typical for the period, and has a bonnet laced to the foot. This bonnet was bent with a "chain" lacing which could be quickly undone if sail had to be reduced. Her oyster boat model made good sense for yachting in the shoal waters of the Delaware. She was a club-owned boat, and her wide, stable decks allowed twenty-odd members to sail aboard with minimal crowding or discomfort. Of course, for racing this hull required a large sail plan, and this, combined with her shoalness, produced a vessel which demanded constant vigilance when sailed in unsettled weather. The following account appeared in the *New York Times* on July 31, 1887:

> Philadelphia. The famous cabin yacht *Minerva*, owned by the Minerva Yacht Club, of this city, was capsized in the Delaware River, off Boulston-street, Camden, this afternoon, and sank. Thomas Kennedy, a member of the club, and William White, the colored steward, were drowned.
>
> The boat left her moorings opposite Federal-street, Camden, shortly before four o'clock, with a delegation of the club bound on their annual cruise . . .
>
> The party intended to sail to New York to witness the coming regatta at Bay Ridge. When below South-street the sky clouded and the rain fell in torrents. Captain Thompson at once ordered sail taken in, and the crew sprang to obey his commands. The peak halyards had swollen with the rain and jammed in the block. At this time a sudden squall struck the boat, and she careened to her starboard side. Before she could be righted she filled, and in a few moments sank.
>
> Most of the party in the cabin having gone there to escape the rain, they scrambled on deck as soon as the boat shipped water, and soon all hands were struggling for their lives in the river. The storm, as described by the men, resembled a whirlwind more than a squall, and the water was very rough.
>
> The tugs *Archambault* and *Minnie*, which had witnessed the upsetting of the yacht, went to the assistance of the men in the water.

The oyster business was very widespread along the eastern seaboard, and the oyster sloop, in many local variations, was probably the most ubiquitous sailing craft on the coast. Most were small, probably closer in size to the stakeboat than to the *Minerva*. Many were inevitably used for pleasure, and many yachts were built to their general model. Both the notorious sandbagger and the traditional big New York sloop yachts had some oyster boat parentage. The most famous ex-oyster sloop yacht was Captain Joshua Slocum's rugged old *Spray*, which took him around the world alone.

Stebbins copy negative 471

The schooner yacht *Coronet*

The big *Coronet* romps in Long Island Sound in 1893, the year she was purchased by Arthur Curtis James. In 1889, under another owner, she had made a world voyage. Under James's flag she continued to be cruised extensively, and made a voyage to Japan, twice rounding Cape Horn, on an unsuccessful attempt to observe an eclipse. (On this voyage the owner's party was picked up and returned at San Francisco.) The *Coronet's* model was evidently developed from pilot schooner design, and she was rigged with the long lowermasts and relatively short topmasts characteristic of pilot schooners.

Captain Christopher Crosby, who had participated in her design and supervised her construction, was a fixture aboard the *Coronet* for many years. Previous to the victory over the *Dauntless* he had cruised the *Coronet* to Cowes in less than eighteen days, and for the Japan expedition he delivered her from New York to San Francisco in 117 days. In addition to being a thorough seaman, Captain Crosby was also something of a character. Such a skipper — usually termed the "sailing master" in deference to the owner's feelings — was a great prize. He provided the guests an intriguing contact with a rough-cut man of the world, and contributed much to their entertainment on a cruise. In various accounts written about the *Coronet* Captain Crosby figures prominently. No doubt he was fully aware of his expected role and enjoyed making the most of it. The sole cabin guest on the return passage from San Francisco, who was apparently shipped as "audience," wrote:

> The captain is a born story-teller. Early a Maine skipper, and a captain of a coasting vessel, drifting into all sorts of enterprises ashore and on the sea, serving a brief war term in the navy, he designed, he says, the *Coronet*, and has captained her under various owners since her launching in '85. Pretty nearly all that the world furnishes to be seen by such a knockabout he has shot keen eyes upon. His opinions are strongly based on some fact, much fancy. The combination makes him whimsical. He is a philosopher and a satirist — yes decidedly a cynic with no reverence for man, none abounding for God. Scorning all pretense and sentiment, counting cleanness of mind the same with Willie-Nillieism, he is a reprobate undenied, yet not altogether hateful. All he has to say comes out with equal force and quaintness. One isn't uncommonly surprised at his illiteracy; but he has a vocabulary that is marvelous. A genius at words, he owns and constantly uses an unabridged compilation of the provincialisms and archaisms of all places in all

times. Joined to Mrs. Malaprop he would have sired a language builder.[21]

Another guest on a previous occasion wrote in his journal: "This morning we find ourselves just out of sight of some islands which are twenty miles from San Francisco Bay. Captain Crosby calls them 'Furlongs' or 'Fallons.' We imagine he may mean 'Farallones.'"[22]

The *Coronet* is still very much afloat, although now fitted with a very reduced rig, as befits a lady of her years. She is maintained at East Gloucester by her long-time owner, The Kingdom, an evangelical missionary church. Under The Kingdom's flag she made a difficult and eventful world voyage from 1907 to 1909.

In light of the *Coronet's* extraordinary voyaging, it is interesting to note that by both reputation and appearance she was a very wet vessel in a seaway. Accounts written by guests fairly drip.

Stebbins copy negative 4418

The sloop *Clytie*

The centerboard sloop *Clytie* in Boston waters, flying the Eastern Yacht Club burgee from her housed topmast. Topmasts were housed in "lower sail" breezes to increase stability and to decrease windage; on even the largest schooner yachts topmasts could be housed or restepped in a matter of minutes with a good crew. A watersail is furled along the underside of the *Clytie*'s boom, and her jib has been set "flying," without a stay.

The *Clytie*'s mainsail is double-reefed, although it is apparent that something less than a gale is blowing; many nineteenth-century yachts probably reefed more often in one season than most modern yachts do in a lifetime. It would appear that the old idea (reflected by racing rules) was to reduce sail as needed, while today just the reverse is the case. One of the reasons behind the preference for large sail plans even on cruising yachts was probably that before the introduction of auxiliary engines yachts spent far more time sailing in light wind.

The *Clytie* was built by the Herreshoffs in 1867. A number of sloops and catboats built by the several Herreshoffs from Bristol were imported to Massachusetts Bay beginning at least in the mid-sixties. They enjoyed a family reputation for speed and innovation. At first glance the *Clytie* resembles the famous *Shadow*, but, although the two were about the same length, the *Shadow* was nearly a foot and a half deeper, and over four feet beamier.

The *Clytie* dates from the beginning of the great surge in American yachting which accompanied the emergence of an enlarged and enriched business class in the post-Civil War decades. New York and Boston were the centers of the growing sport, coinciding with their geography, history, and positions in the worlds of finance and society. Massachusetts Bay was early the home of the largest fleets of owner-sailed racing yachts; by the nineties it had apparently become the most active small boat sailing area in the country. The vitality of yachting has always been based on the health of small boat sailing.

From the mid-sixties onward numerous clubs were organized in the Boston area, and a number of boat builders set up shops. There was very lively interest in yacht design, and the free classes in naval architecture conducted by J. L. Frisbee and sponsored by the City of Boston were enthusiastically attended.[23] Yachting was not restricted to the very well-off, and a number of small racing boats were owned by partnerships of young men. Racing was for cash stakes, and remained so at most clubs at least into the nineties.

As a rough generalization, Massachusetts Bay yachting was divided socially between the Marblehead clubs and the Boston Harbor clubs, the latter claiming, perhaps, a more diverse membership. In part, differences in styles between the North Shore and Harbor clubs reflected their differing home waters. Whereas small Marblehead Harbor opened out to deep, exposed waters, Boston Harbor contained the shoal expanses of Quincy and Hingham Bays, which supported the local contingent of centerboard enthusiasts. Their zeal never approached the extremes of the New York shoal-draft establishment, however, and Massachusetts Bay escaped the full fury of the great cutter-sloop controversy of the eighties. The Boston area had long been home to a fleet of deep pilot schooner-type yachts, as well as many smaller keel sloops. These early keel sloops were generally of shoal-draft model, with inside ballast, and with the addition of a fin-type keel.[24]

The fleet list of the Hull Yacht Club for 1893 gives some indication of the local mix. (The Hull Yacht Club was for some years the most active of the Boston Harbor clubs — its clubhouse may be just glimpsed behind the sail of the catboat at the center of the frontispiece photograph.) The fleet included eighteen steamers, two yawls, twelve keel schooners, two centerboard schooners, thirty-nine centerboard "sloops and cutters," twenty-six keel "sloops and cutters," and thirty-six catboats.[25]

Not all of the yachts listed would actually have been based in Boston Harbor, as some were owned by active yachtsmen who sailed from other clubs and who maintained memberships in several clubs about Massachusetts Bay.

The distinction between sloops and cutters, once as clear as the differences between the Union Jack and the Stars and Stripes, had become very blurred by the early nineties, and some yachts were indeed termed "centerboard cutters."[26]

Stebbins copy negative 57

The schooner yacht *Atalanta* in Long Island Sound

The *Atalanta*, built in 1873, was one of the great fleet of big schooners which crowned New York yachting in the seventies. Her owner, William Astor, is better remembered for his huge steam yacht *Nourmahal* of 1884; the general exodus of the big schooner owners into steam in the early eighties ended the schooner era in American yachting.

While many of the New York schooners were of keel model, the shoal centerboarder was the characteristic type. Since this was before the use of outside ballast with keel models, the centerboarders tended to be faster, and were apparently more comfortable in a seaway (with the board partly down).[27] They were also decidedly more maneuverable, and faster in stays. Reflecting the sandbagger approach to life, the centerboard schooner was developed to extreme proportions, gaining speed at the expense of safety and sanity.

The fundamental (though mistaken) foundation upon which the shoal-draft establishment rested was the belief that it was easier to push a hull over the water rather than through it. Since sail area was not taxed by measurement rules, sail-carrying power was increased by making shoal hulls wider. The result was greater and greater sail areas and wider and proportionately shoaler hulls. The predisposition toward shoal-draft was a result of the obvious advantages of a shoal vessel in shoal waters, the convenience of roomy cabins and wide deck-space (or cabin tops), cheaper construction costs (for sloops, anyway), and long tradition. The big centerboarders possessed tremendous initial stability and no final stability. Up to the point of capsizing their great stiffness could induce a false, and occasionally fatal, sense of security. And for every actual capsizing there must have been countless bad scares which took some of the fun out of sailing.

The decline of the shoal-draft yacht in general, and of the shoal schooner in particular, dated from the 1876 capsizing of the big schooner *Mohawk*, which drowned several people. The *Mohawk* was the extreme ostentatious "skimming dish." She was 121 feet on the waterline, with over thirty feet of beam. She drew but seven feet with the board up, and over thirty-one with it down. Her rig stretched 235 feet from jib boom tip to main boom end, and the top of her main topsail sprit was 163 feet above the water. Through gross negligence (perhaps encouraged by her stiffness) she was caught by a line squall while lying on a short cable with topsails set, and her mainsheet fast.

She was refloated, her rig reduced, and she was used as a coastal survey vessel, a service for which she was well suited.[28]

In 1883 the big schooner *Grayling* was capsized by a squall during her maiden sail. Nobody was drowned, and she was soon back in service. W. P. Stephens happened by and witnessed her awkward predicament: "We sailed back on Sunday, a bright clear day, and when abreast of Hoffman Island sighted the masts of a schooner, the tops just clear of the water and the crew working there to unbend the topsails. They paid no attention to our very foolish question as to the name of the vessel."[29]

Defenders of the type cited the performance of the shoal centerboarder *Vesta* in the famous winter race across the North Atlantic in 1866. They blamed the capsizings on freakish twisters, bad seamanship, or combinations thereof. When the schooner *Agnes* rolled over and sank during a squall while lying at anchor with her sails furled, it was explained that she had not been capsized at all; rather, she had been "undercut."[30]

For their part, many shoal-draft critics mistakenly condemned all centerboard yachts, instead of singling out the extreme offenders of common sense. The centerboard, of course, was a device of proven merit, and in the mid-eighties approximately half of the schooners in the huge Atlantic coasting fleet were moderately shoal centerboarders.

The *Atalanta* is slipping along easily under plain sail, apparently content to let others in the squadron do the racing. She is taking quite a fleet of handsome pulling boats along for the cruise. In real life the racing mark with the flag flying was probably an oyster boat.

Stebbins copy negative 529

Charlie Barr aboard the cutter *Shona*

April 1888

The Scotch "plank on edge" cutter *Shona* fitting out at Lawley's, South Boston. The *Shona* was forty-two feet overall, thirty-three feet on the waterline, with a beam of five feet, eight inches. She drew six feet, four inches. She makes an odd contrast in hull form with the big Burgess-designed sloop *Volunteer*, which is laid up in the basin astern.

The young man with the tam-o'-shanter looks to be young Charlie Barr, the *Shona*'s professional skipper, who as a naturalized citizen, would defend the America's Cup three times. In 1887 the swift *Volunteer* had defended the Cup against the beautiful cutter *Thistle*, the pride of Scotland, which had been sailed by Captain John Barr, Charlie's older half-brother. John received such a cold reception back home in Scotland that he emigrated to Marblehead to continue his career.[31]

Charlie first came to America in 1885 as cook aboard the cutter *Clara*. Later, he became skipper of the little *Shona*, and raced her with success. He studied navigation during the winter in Boston, and in the summer after this photograph was taken he sailed the famous cutter *Minerva* across the Atlantic.

American and British yachts developed toward opposite extremes. As American yachts grew wider and shoaler, British cutters became narrower and deeper. The traditional cutter yacht was descended from the eighteenth-century English Channel revenue cutter. The term "cutter" referred as much to hull form as to rig; essentially, cutters were single-masted, deep-draft vessels suited for service in the rough waters surrounding the British Isles. Their greatest feature was the fact that they were non-capsizable.

For purposes of racing handicapping, British yachts were measured by an ancient system originally devised to provide an estimate of the capacity of River Tyne colliers. This system penalized beam and had the effect of encouraging the construction of narrow, deep hulls. In the early seventies cutter yachts went from an average four beams-to-length to as many as six beams, as the old stability of form was superseded by a stability of weight, with outside ballast hung under the keel. By 1880 the very narrow cutter dominated British racing.[32]

During this period there was a growing disenchantment among some American yachtsmen with the shoal, capsizable, American center-boarder. They became intrigued with the idea of the cutter, which could be cruised in safety, enjoyed rough seas, and did not require an outsized sail plan. The cutter *Madge*, which so caught the centerboarders by surprise in 1881, was apparently shipped to New York with help from the young "cutter cranks" of the Seawanhaka Yacht Club. Their claims of superiority for the cutter were met with derision by the old shoal-draft camp. Inter-racial competition proved that either type could beat the other under the right conditions. The sloops were "drowned" in heavy weather, and on light days with old seas, but could hope to prevail in "normal summer" conditions.

The controversy quickly developed strong patriotic overtones which all but eclipsed the practical considerations. It coincided with the rise of the "anglo-maniacs," status-seeking Americans who aped English manners. One taunting ditty went: "The queer things you see, and the queer things you do,/ Are English you know, quite English, you know."[33]

By all accounts the most insufferable of the cutter cranks was Vice Commodore M. Roosevelt Schyler of the Seawanhaka Club, who was an extremist, and was either blind to the cutter's several faults, or else found them endearing. He kept his cutter *Yolande* (of his own design) in commission through November so that he could brag to sloop men about sailing with snow on deck. Cutters were very wet in a windy chop, and Cary Smith loved to tell of the *Yolande*'s trial sail on such a day. When the proud owner marched up the wharf afterwards an onlooker asked, "How did she go, Robo?" "Dry as a bone," he replied, "not a drop on deck," as rivers of salt water drained from his clothing and flowed out of his shoes.[34]

Stebbins copy negative 1679

The coasting schooner *Lavinia Campbell*

1885

The coasting schooner *Lavinia Campbell* of Greenport, New York, hauled out on the railway of a Chelsea, Massachusetts, shipyard. The *Campbell* was built in 1883 by David Clark on the Kennebunk River, Maine, for employment in the coal trade from Middle Atlantic ports to urban, industrial New England. She was considered one of the fastest and finest of all the many hundreds of three-masters then sailing on the coast.[35] She was a "flush decker," without raised poop or forecastle decks, and with her houses "trunked" down into the main deck.

While the eye is at once caught by the strength and grace of the *Campbell*'s bow, the clean modeling of her afterbody is also worthy of notice. A Stebbins photograph of the *Campbell* under sail shows the proportions of her jib boom to have been distorted but very little by the camera; very long and well-steeved bowsprits and jib booms were characteristic of big Eastern coasting schooners.

The essence of a coasting schooner, of course, was its simple rig. A big 700-ton three-master like the *Campbell* was ordinarily sailed by a crew of eight, all told. Reflecting economies of scale and steam donkey power, the huge 3000-ton five- and six-masters of later years would be manned by crews of eleven to fourteen men.

A society which created a vehicle as marvelous as the *Lavinia Campbell* to carry its coal is also worthy of our consideration — although the plump little catboat hauled out in the foreground is proof that not all vessel builders were as successful or as concerned with achieving the sublime. The large Eastern coasting schooner was in many ways symbolic of the period between the Civil War and World War One, when American society was on the one hand irreversibly committed to a future of vast changes, while on the other still tied to traditions of ages past.

Because coasting schooners were built of wood and propelled by wind, one might expect to find them crude and impractical anachronisms in the rapidly developing New Age of steam power and steel. In fact, coasting schooners served as major carriers of the coal and bulk materials required for the construction and operation of the growing cities, suburbs, railroads, and industries of the Northeast. Schooner design steadily evolved in response to changing demands, and the resulting vessels, in the main, reflected an intelligent and successful approach to the requirements for increased capacity, efficiency, and economy at sea.[36]

The institution of coastal sail was very much interested in the greedy savaging of the magnificent southern pine forests, and in the coal industry, that huge and vital undertaking founded on cynical exploitation of men and land. Coasting schooners also supplied most of the tonnage required by the big ice industry of Maine. No business better illustrates the intriguing economic fabric of the times than wooden, wind-driven schooners, laden with ice harvested from clean rivers, sailing for the urban markets created by industrialism and economic expansion.[37]

In an increasingly complex society, schooner construction and management remained largely small-town, "first name" enterprises. Wooden shipbuilding (particularly in Maine, where schooner construction was centered) was really a folk industry based upon traditional skills, and requiring little capital investment. Schooners were financed individually through the sale of shares to many separate parties; there was no schooner trust. Vessels were modeled by men with no formal training, who depended on native genius rather than advanced mathematical theorems. Coasting schooners always bore the distinctive personal touches of the men who built them.

The business of coasting was an exceedingly hard way of life. The question of how badly the coastal sailor was "used" must be judged in relation to one's notion as to the balance between free will and economic compulsion, and — most importantly — in comparison with the prevailing standards. There is no question but that from the standpoint of conditions today, life aboard even the finest schooner was frequently dangerous and uncomfortable, and that the sailor received little pay for his labors. But low wages and dangerous working conditions were characteristics of many trades ashore, and had always prevailed at sea. The dramatic and pitiful sufferings of shipwrecked mariners were common items in newspapers, particularly in the winter months. The average reader probably took little more notice of drowned sailors than we do today of the grisly details of the vastly greater carnage on the highways.

448

Stebbins copy negative 448

The New York sloop *Daphne*

A delightful photograph of the New York centerboard sloop *Daphne* enjoying ideal sailing. When meeting a despised cutter on a day such as this the *Daphne* might hope to sail the nuisance under.

Vessels should be remembered in company with their home environments. New York sloops were created for sailing in their protected local waters, where they enjoyed a diet of fresh afternoon southerlies. The *Daphne* hailed from the Atlantic Yacht Club at Bay Ridge, Brooklyn, and regularly sported among the constant parade of merchant ships passing in the great roadstead of the Lower Bay. She ventured outside of Sandy Hook on only the fairest of days. For cruising she might run up the mighty Hudson, or head out east to the western reaches of Long Island Sound. The Sound was then the most perfect of yachting grounds. The afternoon breeze had not yet been walled off by the hot convection rising from pavement to windward, and the clean, warm waters were decorated by the sails of coasters and oyster vessels. The shores were yet rural and unspoiled.

The New York sloops were descended from traditional oyster and cargo vessels. In the early seventies the type's predisposition towards beamy shoalness was encouraged by the "cubical content rule," which was based on measurements from the keel rabbet to the lowest level of the sheer, and inspired a class of dangerous and extreme "skimming dishes" and "bowls" with unnaturally low freeboard, big houses, and shoal, broad, short-ended hulls. Sail area went untaxed, and the "dishes" were heavily over-sparred and over-canvassed.[38]

The *Daphne* was completed in 1885, a fateful year. Not only had the cubical content rule already been retired by at least the New York and Seawanhaka Yacht Clubs, but the compromise Cup sloops *Puritan* and *Priscilla*, built under the new Seawanhaka Rule which rendered the old sloops obsolete, were obviously of a superior type. And in September the *Daphne* was defeated in a special sweepstakes with the newly-arrived Scotch cutter *Clara*.

Although the *Daphne*'s tall lowermast, short topmast, and big single headsail (a topsail is set above) were pure essence of sloop, her hull was narrower and deeper than older sloops of her size, reflecting the reluctant acceptance by sloop men that it was possible to have too much of a good thing. Forty-six feet on the water, she was sixteen feet, four inches wide, and drew a little over six feet. The *Fanita*, an 1880 sloop of the same length and considered of the "extreme type," was more than one foot wider and drew five feet. By contrast, the sloop *Coming*, an all-out

"skimming dish" of 1869, was fifty-six feet, ten inches on the waterline, twenty feet, five inches in beam, and drew but four feet, two inches.

The *Coming* is remembered for her survival, adrift and dismasted, in a fierce gale on the Sound in February 1880. This wonder was cited by shoal-draft apologists as proof of the sloop's ability to rally when the chips were really down. Special emphasis was made of the fact that although the brig on which the sloop's crew had regrettably (though understandably) sought refuge was lost with all hands, the dishes of corned beef and cabbage which they had abandoned on the cabin table were not upset. Polemics aside, while such a vessel was no doubt a very determined floater, she soon came unglued if driven in a seaway.[39]

J. Rogers Maxwell, the *Daphne*'s owner, is listed as her designer. She was built by an old-time Brooklyn sandbagger shop, and "designer" probably meant that Mr. Maxwell did most of the talking while Mr. Mumm (or his foreman) did all of the carving and very little listening. Sloops, almost without exception, were "rule of thumbers" built to lines taken off a carved half-model. The *Daphne* was but one in a steady procession of Maxwell-owned yachts, culminating with the magnificent 1906 schooner *Queen*. Maxwell was regarded as one of the "able" yachtsmen of the old order. He was a capitalist involved with railroads and cement.

A writer of the nineties reflected on the passing of the shoal-draft yacht: "It must be freely admitted that for the pure comfort and pleasure of sailing, for an appreciation of the inspiriting motion, as well as for the comfort of increased deck and cabin room, nothing yet has exceeded the form of yacht now falling into disuse . . ."[40]

Stebbins copy negative 481

The armored ram *Katahdin*

February 1893

February 4, 1893, a cold day at the Iron Works, Bath, Maine. The armored ram U.S.S. *Katahdin*, two years a-building, is readied for launching. The cold has apparently slowed the emulsion on Stebbins' plate, and the wind-whipped bunting is expressively blurred.

The *Katahdin* was the first and last vessel of her class. Her construction had been strongly opposed by many in the navy, and she owed her existence to the influential chairman of the Senate Committee on Naval Affairs, Senator Hale of Maine. From at least the time of the Greeks, for better or for worse, politics has been a strong influence on the design of naval vessels.

The type of ram represented by the *Katahdin* was conceived and advanced by Rear Admiral Ammen in the early eighties. During the Civil War steam rams had been used to good effect under certain circumstances, and in later years some European navies had built rams when the technology of armor temporarily outran advances in naval ordnance. Admiral Ammen and his friends saw the ram as an inexpensive and practically invulnerable weapon for the defense of seaports, and called for the construction of a great fleet. One supporter wrote:

> Her engagement with an iron ship of the type of the majority most prized by the transatlantic powers would be analogous to a combat between a swordfish and a whale.[41]

According to another less expert enthusiast:

> The ram itself is nothing more than a powerful projectile and when she rushes through the water at eighteen knots an hour and strikes an object with a force of twenty-thousand tons it is only reasonable to suppose that she will make a hole where she does strike.[42]

Despite the apparent logic of that conclusion, some naval men thought that the maximum speed at which a ram could safely deliver a blow was eight knots, and there was serious question whether a ram could, even at maximum speed, be maneuvered so as to deal her fatal puncture. The history of rams in actual combat showed that in thirty-two attempts to ram where there was searoom, with both the rammer and the rammee under control, none had succeeded.[43] The critics claimed that the coastal defender of the future was the fast torpedo boat, which could even sink a ram. The ram crowd responded, very lamely, that the ram's double hull provided against torpedo attack.

When the *Katahdin* underwent speed trials she proved to be a half knot slower than the contract speed. Evidently seizing upon this opportunity, the government refused to accept her. A special act of Congress was required to put the *Katahdin* in the fleet, thereby saving the Bath Iron Works from ruin.

About 1910 the *Katahdin* was decommissioned for use as a target, albeit a mighty low one.

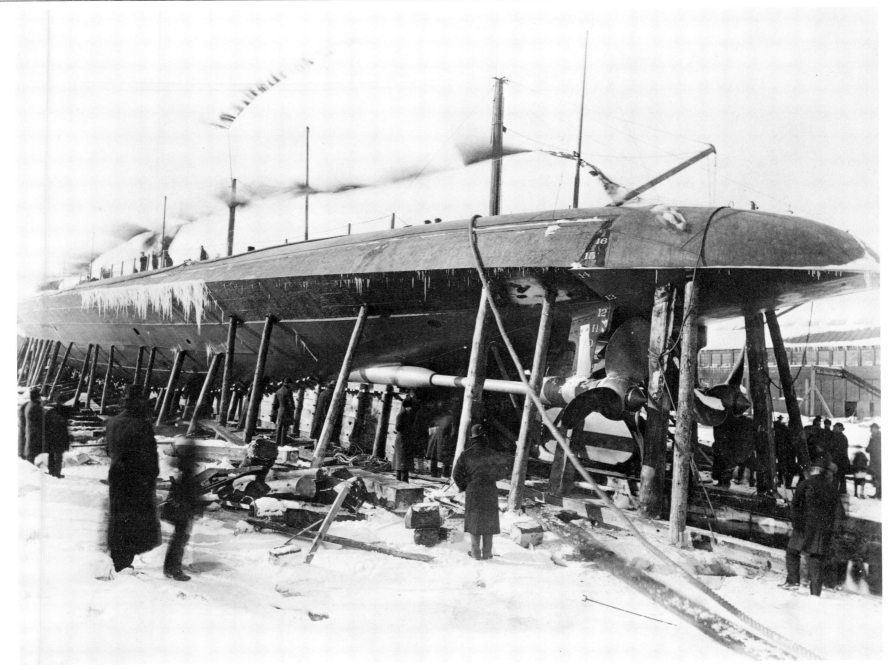

Stebbins copy negative 4274

The Scottish cutter *Clara* in New York Bay

A sailor walks on the *Clara*'s bowsprit footrope, while others on deck are engaged with the cumbersome spinnaker boom. In the background, merchant sailors furl canvas on a full-rigged ship which is likely just in from sea; in a port as alluring as New York sailors vanished quickly, and new crews were not signed on until just before the vessel was towed to sea.

The *Clara* was all cutter. Her rig is strictly regulation, with a short lowermast stepped almost amidships, three headsails, a reefing bowsprit, and the loose-footed mainsail that Americans thought was a disadvantage in a breeze. Designed by William Fife, Jr., she was of partly composite construction with frames of steel and oak, and measured fifty-three feet, seven inches on the waterline, with but nine feet of beam, and nine feet, ten inches "draught." Her twenty-one tons of ballast were all hung outside.

In 1884, her first season of campaigning, she won seventeen of twenty races in home waters. In 1885 she was sailed to America, where she was raced by a Scottish crew under Captain John Barr, a fisherman and boat builder from Gourock. In American waters the *Clara* proved just as formidable, winning all eleven starts in 1886.

So rapid was the improvement in yacht design, however, that by 1891 the once invincible *Clara* could be defeated with ease by even the slowest members of the American "forty-six-footer" class.[44]

Narrow cutters like the *Clara* were very wet and uncomfortable in a seaway, and took particular relish in diving head first into oncoming waves. Quarters were cramped (the "cranks" called them "snug"), and the boats seemed to spend most of their careers sailing on their sides. One can imagine the scorn of the owner of a big, airy, "broad-shouldered" New York sloop peering down into the dark, narrow cabin of the *Clara*. W. P. Stephens recalled:

> I was alongside [the *Clara*] one day in a [sailing] canoe, at the anchorage off Stapleton, Staten Island, for a gam with Captain John; she had lost a bit of her starboard bulwark in a passage around the Cape, and Captain John was fitting in a new piece of teak. There was at that time a New York yacht named *Comfort* (it was said that she was thus named on account of the size of her toilet-room), a messenger boy rowing about hailed "Is this the yacht *Comfort*?" Without raising his eyes from his work or ceasing his hammering Capt. John drawled out in his strong Scotch brogue, "This is na the *Comfort*; this is the *Torment*."[45]

On the day of the photograph there was great interest in New York concerning the trial sail of the America's Cup candidate *Atlantic*, which was the last of the big "rule-of-thumbers." Modeled by Captain Phil Elsworth, who had made his reputation with shoal centerboarders, the half-hearted compromise was to prove a great disappointment.

> N. L. Stebbins, the Boston marine photographer, had a tug down the Bay, to get photographs of the *Atlantic*. After taking a great many from different points of view he ran alongside. It being then after 2 o'clock and there being no sign of wind, Capt. Joe Ellsworth asked Mr. Stebbins to give the *Atlantic* a tow up to Bay Ridge, and that gentleman promptly complied with the request. On the way up Mr. Stebbins entertained the yachtsmen on board the *Atlantic* by showing them proofs of the *Mayflower*, which he had photographed [at Boston] on her trial trip on Sunday.
> *New York Times*, June 1, 1886

The *Mayflower*, of course, defended the Cup against the cutter *Galatea*.

The merchant vessel lying at anchor beyond the *Clara* may be the German ship *Atlantic* — at least, there are eight letters in her name, and the newspapers list the *Atlantic* as arriving at New York that day, twenty-seven days out of Bremen with cement and empty barrels. Some features of her appearance look European, although her "built" wooden masts were typically American. If she is the *Atlantic*, she began life as the ship *Joseph Fish*, and was built at Thomaston, Maine, in 1866. The "barrel trade" of barreled crude oil from New York to Europe employed many German sailing vessels at this time.[46]

Stebbins copy negative 913

The Cunarder *Etruria*

A wonderful photograph of the Atlantic greyhound *Etruria*, eastbound for Liverpool, caught by Stebbins from the westbound *Bothnia*. The bark to leeward appears to have a deckload of lumber. Her signal hoist is doubtless a request to be reported, for she may be at sea a while yet. The lumber bark and the crack Cunarder momentarily share the same piece of ocean, but they exist in very different worlds.

The *Etruria*'s eighteen-knot speed has brought the apparent wind abeam, and her steadying sails are trimmed accordingly. As a breed, the deep and narrow British steamers of this period were famous rollers under the right combination of conditions. The crossed yards reflect old habits, as well as consideration for the passengers' sense of well-being. In the seventies and the eighties broken propeller shafts were a fairly frequent occurrence, and single-screw passenger vessels like the *Etruria* carried some token sail. The broken shaft problem improved through the nineties until the adoption of the McKinley tariffs resulted in a new epidemic among lightly ballasted steamers making heavy weather of it to the westward.[47] Canvas ventilators rise up from the *Etruria*'s deck like hooded cobras.

The liner's forecastle deck is thick with steerage passengers. Fares were cheap, and many may be old immigrants headed home for a summer visit. The photograph was taken near the voyage's end, and they may be gathered forward watching the green coast of Ireland rise out of the sea. Eastbound steerage accommodations were most heavily booked before Christmas, as British tradesmen returned home for the holidays.

The operation of a big liner involved complex social engineering. Although the *Etruria* might have more than 1600 people contained within her 500-foot length, most would have little more than occasional visual contact with persons outside their own group. Members of the two largest groups, the steerage and the saloon passengers, had little in common besides seasickness and the excitement of travel. The 300 crew members, segregated by function into rigid castes, perceived crossings from widely differing perspectives. The stewards, the largest group, probably, save the firemen, lived in a world of soiled cabins and irritable passengers. Theirs was a career in diplomacy. The chefs and bakers were locked in a struggle with astonishing quantities of food, constant deadlines, and rolling stoves. The sailors were the groundsmen of the estate, and their lives of chores were regulated by the boatswain. The oilers and wipers were the serfs in the mystical inner kingdom of steam, a fascinating realm of pulsing power, dancing rods, spinning shafts, noise, heat,

and lubricating oil. And at the foundation of all were the iron men of the North Atlantic, the stokers, laboring with shovel and red-hot slice bar in a special hell of searing heat and roaring furnaces. The *Etruria* burned over 300 tons of coal a day steaming normally; on runs for a record the consumption was greater, and collapsed firemen were lugged out of the stokehold.[48]

Below decks life was hard, life was earnest, and if you had a complaint you could be paid off. Steamship owners, like other shipowners, were generally fitted with hearts of coal. Faithful to tradition, they provided the men with neither bedding nor eating utensils. More to the point, sick stokers labored until they dropped because a missed watch was assigned to others as additional labor, and heaven help the suspected shirker from the displeasure of his mates.

Off watch, the men of the various departments messed and bunked separately from the others. Intercourse between the forces was regulated by custom. The gallery was dependent on the filthy and evil-looking coal trimmers for its supply of stove fuel, and in payment the trimmers carried off the "black pan" containing the leftovers from the cabin. This treasure was, in turn, delivered over to the stokers, who ruled the black gang's mess.[49]

When new in 1884, the *Etruria* and her sister the *Umbria* were the largest and fastest liners on the Atlantic. They were products of the fierce struggle for speed in the New York passenger trade, and within a few years were surpassed, statistically, by bigger twin-screw liners. No vessels, however, were ever more popular or more successful. Although the conditions on the North Atlantic were major factors in the rapid development of steamships, the *Etruria* thrived on the run for twenty-five years.

The Stebbins Collection includes a good selection of views of North Atlantic liners of the period; most are shown under way, in the environs of either Boston or New York harbors.

Stebbins plate 1031

The *Shadow* leads the *Nomad,* as usual

The Cary Smith–designed sloop *Nomad* gives chase to the tireless old *Shadow*. The *Nomad*, which had been altered from centerboard to keel-model, nipped at the *Shadow*'s heels all summer long. Of course, by this date they were both among the "has-beens." In the *Shadow*'s heyday it was said that while some of the competition might keep up with her running downwind, none could touch her going to windward in a breeze. The *Nomad*'s spinnaker has been hoisted in rotten stops, which should part with a sharp tug on the sheet. Setting the sail in this manner kept it from catching on deck and tearing.

The *Shadow* was unusual in that she went fast under six different owners. Like most successful yachts, however, she was apparently always well-managed and well-sailed; it would be difficult indeed to design a boat so superior that she won consistently despite indifferent handling. The *Shadow* went through her first four owners in about as many years before finding young Dr. John Bryant, with whom she stayed for fifteen years. Dr. Bryant had been a noted athlete at Harvard and was a cousin to General Charles Paine, the famed manager of the three Boston America's Cup defenders. Like many leading Boston-area yachtsmen, Bryant bore the name and (presumably) some of the money of an old-time Boston mercantile family. Though founded in the golden age of speculative shipping, these Boston fortunes were sustained in large part through investments in western railroads and other land-bound industries.

The *Shadow*'s racing skipper during the Bryant years (the doctor served as a crew member) was Captain Aubrey Crocker, a native Massachusetts fisherman and boat builder. Under "Arb" Crocker and the famous "*Shadow* crew" the "Boston pet" collected 126 first prizes in 150 starts.[50] Crocker also served as master of Henry Bryant's big sloop *Thetis* and schooner *Alert*.

It was said that Boston yachtsmen tended to interpret racing rules rather more freely than New Yorkers did, especially at starts. Arb Crocker must have been the outlaw among the outlaws, since a New York yachting reporter gossiped that "Capt. Crocker had the reputation down East of taking unwarranted risks for the sake of position."[51] In 1885 he was selected to skipper General Paine's Cup defender *Puritan*, and although the *Puritan* won the series, Arb is best remembered for his misjudgment at the start of the second attempted race which broke the *Genesta*'s bowsprit. The *Puritan* was attempting to cross the cutter's bows, but her mainsail didn't quite make it. The error has been laid to Crocker's long familiarity with the small, maneuverable *Shadow*, and to his lack of experience contending with thirty-foot bowsprits.

They say that the race between the schooners *Iroquois* and *Marguerite* was not a fair test, because "Ned" Willard of this city and Capt. Aubrey Crocker of Cohasset helped sail the *Marguerite* . . . The owner of the *Iroquois* seems to be of the opinion that nobody on earth can defeat the two skippers in question, and he wants to race again, but with less experienced competitors.
New York Times, August 30, 1891

The *Shadow*'s long rule was ended in 1887 by the Burgess sloop (or cutter) *Papoose*, which had been designed for the young Adams brothers with that goal in mind. Although termed a "compromise," the *Papoose*'s model combined the wide beam of the sloop with the deep keel and outside ballast of the cutter, and would seem to have been derived mostly by way of straight addition. She was thus of very great power, requiring a large and unhandy racing sail plan. Charles Francis Adams recalled her debut:

Our first race was off Nahant. Burgess came along with a double interest, because he feared that if we showed speed, *Thistle*, representing the same idea, might take the America's Cup from *Volunteer*. He was wrong as to the Cup, but he was right in thinking that the reign of the centerboard type ended that day.[52]

The *Shadow* was decisively beaten. Her only consolation was that her old rival, the cutter *Shona*, was "nowhere at all."

51

The steam yacht *Admiral*

1892

The *Admiral* was owned by a Providence horseshoe manufacturer, and is shown steaming out the East Passage, at Newport. She was the last vessel designed by D. J. Lawlor, who was said to have designed 179 steamers in addition to many hundreds of sailing craft.[53] Although handsomer than many, the *Admiral* suffers from the "whole not being the sum of the parts" syndrome which affected many American steam yachts. Her rather weak bow was of a style once in vogue with big American iron yachts and coastal steamers. Her crossed yard is intended primarily for decoration, as is the foolish little bowsprit set above an extravagance of scrollwork. The elevated helm is probably quite practical, but it looks slightly ridiculous. The deckhouse, however, has been handled with rare restraint. A yacht this size could certainly carry a much larger house, although a structure of "standing" height would have been out of scale with her general proportions.

In fairness to Dennison Lawlor, it should be recorded that she was built after his death. Of prime importance is the fact that she probably looked very much better below the waterline, and was easily driven. Many of the more questionable details of a steam yacht's appointment were often specified by the owner, and when taking into account the *Admiral's* pretentious name and straw-hatted deckhand, one suspects that she may have got off lightly at that. Like most American steam yachts she had a light, quick-firing water-tube boiler and a compound engine.

For several decades steam yachts were all the rage among the carriage trade, and one cannot fail to be impressed by the large number which appear in the Stebbins Collection. Apparently they were a bread-and-butter item for a marine photographer. The growth of steam yachting may have been the principal cause for the retarded development of wholesome sailing yachts, particularly in the New York area, where the favored cruising grounds lay out through a long tidal river. A fast steam yacht was just the thing for the busy man with many appointments to keep, and their increased popularity spelled the end for the great class of New York schooner yachts of the seventies. Probably a major reason behind the New York Yacht Club's less than urgent attitude towards the reform of the measurement rules in the nineties was the fact that the owners of the big racing sloops cruised aboard their steamers.[54]

A New York steam yachtsman of the eighties described the situation:

Your regular old yachtsman has a profound contempt for steam yachts. He considers that all the romance and pleasure of yachting consist in the uncertainties, dangers, and difficulties attending sailing. He glories in the storms which compel the shortening of sail, the lying-to, the scudding before the wind under a staysail, and all the other vicissitudes which attend excess of wind; while, on the other hand, he takes dead calms, with sails idly flapping against the masts . . . with philosophy and contentment, passing the long hours of inaction in spinning yarns and (possibly) drinking cocktails. This class of yachtsmen is slowly passing away, and is being succeeded by men of more modern views. Gradually we see some of these gentlemen disposing of their sloops and schooners and ordering steamers to replace them . . .

The great truth is gradually dawning on the minds of yachtsmen that steam is the perfect motive power. Steam yachtsmen can go where they please and when they please, and, what is more important, *they know when they will get back.*

In this happy country, we are nearly all men of business, and we have neither time nor inclination to be becalmed on the glassy ocean for hours and days, or to creep along at three knots indefinitely . . .[55]

Stebbins copy negative 4155

Three Burgess sloops

The sloops *Milicete, Gossoon,* and *Wayward,* all designed by Burgess, and all built by Lawley, during a race off Marblehead.

Edward Burgess of Boston was a trained entomologist who was forced by a financial reversal to turn to his hobby of yacht designing for a living. As an architect he was largely self-taught, and depended more heavily on art than science. A trip to Scotland made him something of a cutter crank, while at home he was a great admirer of Herreshoff's old *Shadow.* These influences were joined in his fertile mind and resulted in the great development of the "compromise" model yacht. In the seven years preceding his death at the age of forty-three he produced 137 designs, including three America's Cup defenders, steam yachts, schooner yachts, coasters, and fishermen. His vessels were characterized by singular beauty.[56]

The *Gossoon,* behind the committee tug, was the third "forty-footer" (waterline length) designed by Burgess for Charles and George Adams. The first, the famous *Papoose,* was the original of the class. The forties were the most popular "open" class intended for cruising as well as racing, and almost all of the best boats were Burgess-Lawley creations. While the *Papoose* had been designed to defeat the old *Shadow,* the *Gossoon* was intended to humble the Fife cutter *Minerva,* which had routed the American boats in 1889. In 1890 the *Gossoon* and the *Minerva* (the latter was sailed by the professional Barr brothers) fought fiercely to a tie, and killed further interest in the class. The new boats ordered that year were for the new forty-six foot class.

The *Milicete* was an early centerboard-model forty-six-footer. She did well enough in 1890, but was outclassed by the new boats in 1891. The nine boats that were added that year (five were Burgess designs) cost altogether $100,000, and all would be outclassed after that season.[57] The sensation was the innovative *Gloriana,* designed by Nat Herreshoff, who had returned to designing racing yachts after a long absence devoted to steam. In 1892 his fin-keeler *Wasp* outclassed even the *Gloriana.* Between the financial burden of building new yachts and the physical difficulties of handling the large, competitive sail plans, the growing movement towards restricted-design and one-design classes is easily understood.

Edward Burgess died of typhoid fever and overwork in July 1891, shortly before the *Gloriana* rendered his newest boats obsolete. In appearance Burgess and Herreshoff were somewhat similar, and both were the same age, but in temperament and approach to designing they were very different. It was Burgess' custom to perform a few cartwheels on deck whenever one of his yachts finished first.[58] Nat Herreshoff would have sooner drowned himself.

George Lawley & Son of City Point were the leading Boston yacht builders. Old George came from England; young George F. ran the yard from 1879 until 1920. He came to prominence building the first two Burgess Cup sloops, providing the technical expertise Burgess lacked. An able designer, he was known for his high standards and great warmth.[59]

In 1890 Charles Francis Adams was just out of Harvard, and was already an expert helmsman. He and his brother George were leaders in the "forties" and the "forty-sixes." In later years he would skipper an America's Cup defender, serve as the Secretary of the Navy, and become Boston's leading citizen. He was a very intense and scientific sailor, and his demeanor during a race was said to be that of a "man burying the dead." (Charlie Barr, by contrast, sailed a race showing all the concern of a man enjoying a picnic.) Nevertheless, the young Adamses who later regularly crewed for him served with cheerful devotion.[60]

Most yachtsmen have had enough after racing over the outside course, and pick up mooring and go ashore forthwith; not so Charley Adams. As soon as the finish line is crossed, and a cruising mainsail and jib substituted for the racing set, he picks up his tender and starts from Marblehead towards Minot's Light, and when the wind is light it is sometimes long after midnight before he gets to his moorings at the "Glades," Cohasset.[61]

The royal tender *Elfin* at Cowes

1886

Cowes, Isle of Wight, England. The royal tender *Elfin*, built at Chatham Dockyard in 1849, paddles serenely before a refined landscape. The estate on the hill is Osborne House, Queen Victoria's favorite residence, overlooking the Medina River. The delightful little *Elfin* wears her age most gracefully, a reflection, no doubt, of her diagonal mahogany planking and other manifestations of the Admiralty's concern regarding the construction and maintenance of a royal craft. The *Elfin* served as one of the two tenders for the big royal yachts *Osborne* and *Victoria & Albert*, and at the annual review of the fleet at Spithead she traditionally maintained station on the *V & A*'s port quarter.[62] Queen Victoria enjoyed the privacy aboard her steam yachts, and helped make this form of yachting stylish.

Cutters are hoisted port and starboard, and the *Elfin*'s crew must include picked oarsmen. The pilot stands on a true bridge connecting the two paddle boxes, while the helmsman steers from the very stern. Communication was presumably effected by means of a subtle semaphore system of raised eyebrows and crooked fingers. The two telegraphs on the bridge indicate that the paddles could be worked independently, which would be a very great advantage considering her leanness. Artful sparring gives her an air of great lightness, which is complemented by the raked and belled stack. Although spiritually the *Elfin* must belong with the great British steam yachts, she would appear to be a more direct predecessor to the admirable river and estuary excursion steamers built towards the end of the century.

Stebbins' trip to England combined business and pleasure. He published many of his photographs of English yachts the following year in his lavishly-produced album, *American and English Yachts*. This was a timely work, appearing while the cutter-sloop issue was still warm, and at an active and interesting period of America's Cup racing. The book was introduced by a highly readable treatise on the state of yacht design written by Edward Burgess, who was then at the peak of his powers and popularity.

C. J. C. McAlister described the scene at the Cowes Regatta in the mid-eighties:

> This is by many regarded as the great aquatic carnival of the year. Nevertheless, the racing is usually of the tamest possible description, as for several of the events — notably the race for the Queen's Cup — members only are permitted to enter. This club is perhaps the least representative of all the yachting associations in England, and if the interests of the pastime were left solely in its hands, yachting would have sunk to a low ebb indeed. The members form a curious combination of "swells" and "snobs." The former, with the Prince of Wales at their head as commodore, are generally smart yachtsmen, but the latter, unfortunately, preponderate, which probably accounts for the curious manner in which the affairs of the club are managed.[63]

The Stebbins Collection contains several views of Cowes Roads at Regatta time, as well as many fine portraits of leading English yachts. The abundant wealth and leisure-time of the English upper classes supported the greatest fleet of big yachts in the world. In 1886 Lloyd's Register listed 409 British steam yachts. Twenty years later the fleet had grown to 1,558, of which twenty-six were in excess of one thousand tons. By way of contrast, the 1906 list included 193 American steam yachts, of which four were larger than one thousand tons.

Stebbins plate 1021

The schooner yacht *Gitana* Down East

The keel schooner *Gitana* on a cruise Down East, anchored just to the west of the steamboat landing at North Haven, along the Fox Island Thorofare. The mast of a cutter-rigged yacht rises beyond her; astern we see the mainsail of a little schooner-rigged fishing boat. The house on the bluff must be the summer cottage of one of the island's wealthy Boston rusticaters, since no local would care to challenge winter from such an exposed location. The sailors of the *Gitana* have rigged a fringed awning to keep the fog that will condense on the main rigging from dripping on the afterdeck. The long spinnaker pole is hoisted along the foremast.

The *Gitana* was the outstanding Boston schooner yacht of her time. Modeled and built by D. J. Lawlor at East Boston in 1882, she was owned by William F. Weld, a grandson of the famous Boston shipowner of the same name. Her rig, with a shortened foremast, was something of a departure locally, and was one of the few features of yacht rigging to be adopted by the fishermen.[64]

About 1885, Dr. Charles Weld, the owner's brother, visited North Haven as a guest aboard the *Gitana*. He fell in love with the island, and inspired the growth of its unique summer colony. One of the *Gitana*'s boats was used as a model for the famous North Haven dinghys, which remain the oldest American racing class.

The *Gitana* was cruised extensively, and voyaged to the Mediterranean and the Caribbean. Although never campaigned grimly, she did well enough when raced. The Stebbins Collection contains a number of excellent photographs of her. Views of her deck and cabin are included in *Portrait of a Port: Boston, 1852–1914*, by W. H. Bunting.

The *Gitana*'s best-known skipper was Captain Ed Sherlock of South Boston, who was known as a "navigator," meaning that he was capable of performing celestial observations.[65] No doubt many captains of large sailing yachts could not. Most sailing masters, whether they came from Down East, Cape Cod, Long Island, Scotland, or Norway, appear to have originated from the ranks of watermen, with backgrounds of fishing, boatbuilding, and coasting. They were generally not deep-water mariners, but were fundamentally small boat sailors. Although the opportunities in the regular merchant marine were sparse, few men who had ever ruled as master or mate aboard a large commercial sailing vessel would be temperamentally suited for the inevitable subservience to owner and guests and the silly games of yachting etiquette that a sailing master had to tolerate. Most of the licensed captains of big steam yachts, particularly after the turn of the century, appear to have been foreign born.

Cruising the cold waters of Maine in the late nineteenth century was a special joy. The coast abounded in unique and unspoiled natural surroundings while yet supporting an intelligent and resourceful population of farmers, fishermen, shipbuilders, and sailors. Most coastal men were skilled in several callings and numerous activities — there may be a few Down Easters aboard the *Gitana*. Despite the close proximity to Boston by water, Maine coastal communities remained socially insular, and the inhabitants were often so thoroughly Yankee as to seem slightly foreign. The principal souvenirs taken home by cruising yachtsmen were countless tales of humorous dealings with the quaint but clever folk ashore. "Having learned that every visit to shore led to some amusing incident, we took our milk can and rowed to the sardine factory wharf . . ."[66]

Stebbins copy negative 1866

The big British cutter *Galatea*

The British cutter *Galatea* weighs her anchor for the second race of her America's Cup challenge. The Cup was easily defended by the compromise sloop *Mayflower*, of Boston.

The *Galatea* had no chance against the faster stripped-down centerboarder, which was raced with grim efficiency under General Paine's management. The *Galatea* was raced in a more relaxed fashion. Her owner, Lieutenant Henn (who had made a name for himself in the Royal Navy chasing slavers on the coast of Zanzibar) and her skipper, Captain Dan Bradford, were strictly cruising men. The cutter raced with all her heavy cruising furnishings aboard, in addition to Mrs. Henn, her dogs, and a monkey. The Henns spent much of every year aboard their cutter, which, like many big English yachts, wintered on the Mediterranean.

The steel *Galatea* was a fine example of the big, narrow, first-class English cutter of the day. Typically, she was superbly finished. She steered with a long tiller, and wide channels were fitted to her hull to give her main shrouds a wider base of attachment. Her designer, John Beavor-Webb, is best known for designing J. P. Morgan's great steam yacht *Corsair*.

With their low initial stability, the narrow cutters were infamous heelers, and when heeled they carried a nasty lee helm. This attribute was most disconcerting to the uninitiated, and did not help their performance to windward. W. P. Stephens described a sail on the *Galatea* in a breeze off Marblehead:

> The rounding of the first mark was a picture still distinct before me, as the jib topsail was broken out the yacht heeled as only a cutter could; the topsail yards were lashed along the port side of the companion and skylights, the weather side as it happened; and I stood on them, looking down over the rail into a deep gulf below the weather quarter. Looking inboard, far below me stood Captain Dan, on the bulwarks rather than on the deck, the water swirling up to his knees, the tiller, a 15-foot steel tube, was high above him, near where I stood, and as he looked up he hauled hard on the relieving tackle to bring her into the wind.[67]

The British yacht owner, or "sportsman," considered his paid hands, called "yachtsmen," to be the finest sailors in the world.

> British yachtsmen of to-day are the result of a long and careful process of selection. They are recruited from among the smartest members of the fishing and other seaside portion of the popula-
> tion . . . He fully appreciates . . . that he may frequently have to spend a considerable number of minutes on a stretch, up to his waist in water, in the lee scuppers, or out on the end of the bowsprit in a seaway . . . In the winter season some may, as they term it, "go steamboating" for a trip or two, but they far more frequently, at their native villages, wile away the time with a little fishing or piloting . . . they are in fact a distinct class, and differ materially from the ordinary fishermen and the crews who man vessels of merchant service . . . The merchant sailor who may have been shipped on an odd occasion as an "extra hand" on board a racing craft expresses his objections to yacht racing with a candor and emphasis characteristic of his profession.[68]

The decisive America's Cup victories of the Burgess-designed keel centerboarders *Puritan* and *Mayflower* in 1885 and 1886 helped persuade the British to reform their measurement rules, allowing for yachts of greater beam. The 1887 Cup challenger *Thistle* and the celebrated "forty-footer" *Minerva* were outstanding examples of the improved type of cutter which resulted.

Stebbins copy negative 1144

The racing catboat *Harbinger*

The big "jib and mainsail" racing cat *Harbinger* slips along in Boston Harbor. The cat boat, in many varieties, was probably the most popular American yacht type during the great surge of recreational boating in the late nineteenth century. Big cat-rigged party-boats and smaller rental cats were common features of seaside resorts. Lewis Herreshoff wrote in the nineties, ". . . for the pleasure of sailing on the usually smooth waters of our sheltered bays, and wafted by the moderate breezes that are most frequently found, nothing can surpass for pure enjoyment the cat-boat of moderate size, say, about 25 feet."[69]

The racing cat, a natural outgrowth of the times, was an animal of a very different stripe from the ubiquitous cat-rigged daysailer. Whereas the working and family cats were generally characterized by fundamental simplicity of rig and personality, the racing cat was a short-tempered breed of vessel which demanded strength, skill, and constant attention from her handlers. Many — particularly those from the New York area — were but little removed from the old outlawed sandbaggers. Racing cats were fitted with outsized sail plans, and on some boats the mainboom overhung the stern by a dozen feet or so. Reefing was sometimes best accomplished from a tender. The *Harbinger*'s boom was forty-feet long, which was as long as her mast. Her gaff was twenty-eight feet long, three inches longer than her waterline length. She was thirteen and a half feet wide. Jibs were fitted — in the sandbagger tradition — in an attempt to balance the ever-larger mainsails. In the wake of the radically-designed sloop *Gloriana*'s success, many racing cats were disfigured by horrible spoon bows.[70]

The *Harbinger* was a Cape-type cat. The Cape cats were developed directly from the big, able fishing cats indigenous to Cape Cod waters. (At least one successful Boston-area racing cat was made over from a regular Chatham fisherman.) With her characteristically high Cape-style bow, even an extreme sail-carrier like the *Harbinger* could be sailed without shrouds, her heavy spruce mast being sufficiently supported by the exaggerated "bury" from the step to the partners.

The *Harbinger* was the first of C. C. Hanley's Cape cats to enter the hot Massachusetts Bay catboat fleet. Charley Hanley of Monument Beach on Buzzard's Bay (he later moved to Quincy) was something of a local figure. In addition to creating big, swift, and handsome catboats, he had been a village blacksmith and was a former piano-maker. He was a self-taught designer, and his big racing cats were said to steer beautifully — no small praise when speaking of catboats.

The *Harbinger* arrived in the summer of 1889, and not only quickly dispatched the local catboat competition, but humiliated two crack "thirty-footer" cutters in a rattling northeaster off Marblehead, despite being more than two feet shorter on the waterline. While beating both, boat for boat, she actually outpointed and outsailed one going to windward. John Hyslop, the respected yacht designer who was serving as measurer for the New York Yacht Club, had come to Marblehead to observe the work of the sensational Scotch cutter *Minerva*, but he went home apparently even more impressed by the deeds of the *Harbinger*. "The *Minerva* has given us some instruction, certainly, but that Cape boat — her performance is something extraordinary."[71]

The following summer the *Harbinger* was deposed by the new Hanley cat *Almira*. Other Cape cats followed, and Hanley boats remained at the head of the Massachusetts Bay catboat fleet.

The Stebbins Collection contains many outstanding catboat photographs. A good selection has recently been included in John Leavens' *The Catboat Book* published by International Marine in 1973. Mr. Leavens is to be congratulated for giving Nathaniel Stebbins credit for his photographs — a courtesy which has long been neglected.

Stebbins copy negative 5842

New Yorkers at an America's Cup Race

Members of the New York Yacht Club Race Committee man their post aboard the big coastal tug *Edgar F. Lukenbach*, which has been chartered as a stake boat. The stake boat set out the windward mark, then maintained station close by. Two mark rafts are on the stern. A large white steam yacht and a chartered tug, with awnings, drift in the background.

The delegation aboard the *Lukenbach* is doubtless composed of prominent and wealthy men. It is a pity we don't know who they are; one was perhaps acquainted with Stebbins. They appear to have had the deckhands remove the heavy horizontal crosspiece of the big towing bitts to provide the white-coated steward with a secure base for his vital tasks. The towboat men, their realm invaded, have retreated forward for the duration.

The New York Yacht Club was a unique institution. Organized in 1844, it was for many years the only yacht club in the country. It maintained its position as America's most influential yachting organization through the sheer prominence of its membership, even after it had become more of a social institution than a society of sailing yachtsmen. As a group, the members took themselves very seriously, and not without reason; if their combined power and influence in 1893 could have been measured it would certainly have rivaled that of the Congress. Indeed, in 1895 one member, J. P. Morgan, arranged to preserve the United States Government itself from a serious financial embarrassment, for which he accepted a generous fee. The club fleet numbered not only most of the largest yachts in the country, but also certainly the smallest proportion of owner-sailed yachts of any club. It included a large number of steam yachts.

The history of the New York Yacht Club is closely identified with the competition for the America's Cup. The Cup itself, of course, has always remained within the Club's tenacious grip, although on three occasions it was defended by Boston boats. The history of these races has been recounted far too often to be repeated here, but it is appropriate to this photograph to take note of the fact that the club's stewardship of the Cup was frequently criticized, particularly on several occasions around the turn of the century. Clinton Crane, who was contemporary to some of these disputes, described the situation.

America's Cup racing has seldom been conducive to good sportsmanship. The attitude of the New York Yacht Club and of its flag officers and committees, and of the actual management of the defenders, has been more that of a man in the forward position at war who has been ordered to hold his position at all costs — at all costs. This had led to numerous incidents and considerable hard feelings.

One of the club's most outspoken opponents was Thomas W. Lawson, an eccentric Boston stock plunger who had made a quick killing as a bear on Wall Street. He was not popular with certain members of the club, and they initially refused to allow his contender, the *Independence*, to compete in the 1901 trials. Lawson blamed the club's unsportsmanlike conduct on its alleged takeover by representatives of the "mushroom aristocracy" of recently-enriched speculators, packing-house owners, and other such social climbers. His description of the enemy is a wonderful exercise in inspired animosity, and a sample sentence is included here to impart the flavor of the dispute:

Natural cowards, queer in body and perverted in mind because of a vicious or low order of ancestry and habit, they could not take an active part in those things which have for their foundation courage, manliness and well-proportioned bodies, and their wealth could not buy, their cunning steal nor their power seize these things which Nature alone can give.[73]

As but one indication that the club was at least not composed entirely of such degenerates, it could be mentioned that Elbridge Gerry, the popular and socially prominent commodore when the photograph was taken, was a forceful pioneer in the movement to prevent cruelty to children, for which he suffered much public abuse from those who felt that he was infringing upon the God-given rights of parents.

Stebbins copy negative 4649

The Boston pilot schooner *Friend*

1888

The new pilot schooner *Friend* looks to be a friend indeed, and she proved to be a fast, handy, and loyal little vessel. The Boston Pilots were good customers of Stebbins, and many prints and plates of pilot schooners are in the collection. They are all fine photographs — it would be difficult to take a bad portrait of a pilot schooner — and some are outstanding.

The blue and white pilot flag, flying from a bamboo pole, is hoisted to the *Friend*'s main truck. The number 7 on her mainsail differentiates her from other schooners in the Boston Pilots' employ. Passengers on transatlantic steamers were commonly encouraged to participate in pools based on the number of the pilot schooner which would meet them. Over a period of time an unscrupulous steamer master, secretly betting through shills, could profitably influence the results.

With a registered length of sixty-seven feet, the *Friend* was unusually small for a pilot schooner built in 1888, when speed had become a prime consideration. Piloting at Boston was a competitive monopoly, and the various schooners often raced each other to put a pilot aboard an eligible vessel. Competition was fiercest for big British steamers, since they drew the most water and consequently paid the highest rates. The explanation for the *Friend*'s size was that she was built to the order of a semi-retired pilot who wished to cruise only in the summer, when pickings were easier, with a complement of other old pilots. They were primarily interested in having a suitable offshore resort where they could drink their whiskey and smoke their cigars in peace.[74]

In later years the *Friend* was purchased by Captain Thomas Cooper, a full-time pilot, who kept her at sea the year around. She had been very heavily constructed, and proved able in all weather. Although he grew very fond of her, the demands of the business eventually forced him to contract for a larger schooner.

Charles Lampee, Captain Cooper's grandson, occasionally made summer cruises aboard the *Friend*.

Perhaps it was on another cruise, I am not certain, that we had put pilots on incoming craft leaving the Skipper [Captain Cooper] the sole remaining pilot on board. His penchant was off-shore cruising, the farther the better. So the boat was headed east by south and was perhaps one hundred and fifty to two hundred miles from Boston Light when a sail was descried astern, heading our way. This was late in the morning and by noon we made her out to be the pilot boat *Varuna* number 6. The *Friend* with all sail set was no slouch, but neither was the *Varuna*. A stern chase is a long chase but number 6, a larger and more powerful boat, was slowly but gradually overhauling us. By the middle of the afternoon we figured that barring a miracle she would overtake us. The miracle happened! The man on the main crosstrees suddenly sung out, "A steamer to the norrard!" The glass showed a large steam yacht, painted white, barkentine rigged, bound in. We kept our course, the *Buffalo* of the Wilson Line, a four master with square yards on her foremast, a signal yard on her main, was momentarily expected to heave in sight. Apparently misled by the yacht's rig the *Varuna* changed her course and set her huge pilot flag. This was indeed a respite, for not long afterwards the *Buffalo* did come into view, dead ahead, and we in turn set our flag, and were gratified when she answered with her jack at the fore. The *Varuna* was now far astern to the norrard, her flag still flying, for by this time she must have also made out the *Buffalo*. When the steamer stopped her engines ready to pick up our pilot the Skipper then offered a bit of masterly advice. As he prepared to get into the canoe he said to the boatkeeper, "Joe, I understand the captain of this ship is supposed to favor the underdog," pointing to the *Varuna* with pilot flag flying. "Now you heave to right across his bow so he won't have a chance to change his mind without running you down."[75]

"Canoe" was the term for the two small rowing boats used for actually delivering and picking up the pilots. One of the *Friend*'s canoes is towing astern on a painter, while the other is on deck. With two canoes aboard, there was always one to leeward which could readily be launched. The "boatkeepers" were the regular sailors on the schooner, the "first boatkeeper" taking command for the trip home after the last pilot had boarded a ship.

I have never seen a list of the various pilot schooners designed and in some cases built by Dennison J. Lawlor of East Boston, but the appearance of the *Friend* indicates that she is his work. He was a firm believer in deep models, and the fine performance of his pilot schooners was an important factor in persuading the fishermen to accept deeper fishing schooners. It would be interesting to know whether the *Friend*'s model still exists.

Stebbins copy negative 1704

The Down East steamer *State of Maine*

The International Line steamer *State of Maine*, operated to St. John, New Brunswick, and other eastern ports, returns once again to Boston, as she had for nearly twenty summer seasons. Amidships, her massive iron walking beam pumps tirelessly away, transmitting the vertical stroke of a single giant piston to the crank of the paddle-shaft, pausing just perceptively every time the crank passes dead center. Her big old-style, non-feathering paddle-wheels churn out a wide wake of froth. The after range lantern is still hoisted on the mainstay after a damp night of steaming across the cold Gulf of Maine. A cook stands in the gangway. Breakfast is over, and most of the passengers are in their cabins packing.

During the period of Stebbins' career the Atlantic seaboard was served by an extensive system of coastal steamship lines. The gaps left by the abandonment of these lines, occurring mostly in the thirties, have never been satisfactorily filled. The majority of the major lines had terminals at either New York or Boston, and Stebbins photographed steamers at both ports. Enough of these photographs have survived to form one of the major historical strengths of the collection. Included are steamers of the Merchants and Miners Line, the Savannah Line, Boston & Bangor, Kennebec, Portland, International, Metropolitan, Eastern, Morgan, Winsor, Clyde, Dominion Atlantic, and others. Most of the surviving photos are simple exterior profiles similar to the example reproduced here. In the *State of Maine*'s particular case, however, there also exist several views taken aboard showing her cabins, engine room, and officers. Three of these have been published in *Portrait of a Port*, while Stebbins' photographs of the spectacularly elaborate interiors of Fall River Liners have appeared (without credit) in many publications.

Stebbins was a familiar figure to anyone with business in Boston Harbor, and the *State of Maine*'s officer, leaning out of the pilot house window with a megaphone, may have just shouted a greeting over the "rapid plowter"[76] of her paddles. To a modern mariner, the roof of her pilot house looks disturbingly naked, being without radar, loran, and radio antennae. Her chief aides to navigation are a compass, a watch, and her pilots' great competence and good fortune. Her humorless-looking bow has no doubt scraped along the sides of several defenseless schooners in her long career of steaming through cold and fog-covered waters.

The *State of Maine*'s route was entirely deep-water, and there was no good reason, beyond force of habit and lower construction costs, to justify her vulnerable traditional design. Sidewheelers had the advantage of quick stopping ability and simple machinery requirements, but their overhanging guards were dangerously exposed to heavy seas. In recognition of this weakness, the *State of Maine*'s guards are narrower than was usual, while her framing, sponsons, and general scantlings were heavier than was customary. Her high superstructure offered great windage, and her wooden construction was always subject to fire. The line built a wooden propeller steamer for the very much reduced winter schedule.

Despite her disastrous potentialities, the *State of Maine* was a long-lived, successful, and popular vessel, and was a very handsome representative of her type. Although built, in large part, to serve the growing summer tourist business, she and her sisters undoubtedly earned more from freight revenues than from passengers.[77] As with the other steamers running to Maine and the Maritimes, she was a very important social and economic link between isolated eastern populations and the Boston area.

The steamer lines which ran to the south from Boston and New York operated fleets of modern, steel-propeller vessels. These lines carried more freight and fewer passengers, and their routes included the frequently rough waters off Cape Cod and the Middle Atlantic capes. Big side-wheelers flourished on Long Island Sound, the Hudson River, Chesapeake Bay, and other sheltered inland waters.

Stebbins plate 12497

The sloops *Gracie* and *Katrina*

The venerable New York sloop *Gracie*, foreground, in a losing cause, sailing against the two-year-old compromise centerboarder *Katrina* in the seventy-foot class during a race off Newport.

Built at Nyack in 1868, the *Gracie* lasted until 1910, and was one of several much-maligned old New York sloops to achieve an advanced age. Structurally, her longevity was probably related to the numerous alterations and half-dozen or so rebuildings which she required to keep in step with changing rules and newer competition. The *Gracie* we see here has been lengthened, "raised up," "hipped out," and given a fashionable overhanging stern and some outside ballast. Her old sloop rig has been changed to the "cutter rig" with divided headsails.[78]

Racing yachts were frequently altered during their lives. In a process of trial and error, it was common practice to reshape a vessel which failed to realize expectations. In the early 1900's some yachts which had been built to rate under the old Seawanhaka Rule had their bows altered to cope with new rule changes. Once past their prime, most big sloops — the *Katrina* would be one, the *Gracie* was an exception — were rerigged as more easily managed schooners.

The *Gracie* was modeled by one Abraham Schank, who ran a paint store. In her original form she undoubtedly bore a strong family resemblance to the big Hudson River and New York Bay cargo sloops. The "waterline area rule" then in effect contained massive potential loopholes, but apparently was not cheated upon.[79] The *Gracie*'s original draft of four feet, eight inches was not rule-inspired.

The steel *Katrina*, a compromise centerboarder, was built under a version of the 1883 Seawanhaka Rule. The Seawanhaka Rule, with many local variations of detail, was the first general measurement formula adopted by multiple clubs, from New York to Boston. The rule attempted to rate yachts according to waterline length and sail area, which were seen as the principal factors in determining speed. It was intended to foster a more wholesome breed of yacht. Although flawed by a fundamental loophole, it did inspire the construction of some very fine yachts, particularly in its first ten years or so.

The *Katrina* was designed by A. Carey Smith of New York, who was one of the ablest yacht designers of the time. In his early years he served as a moderating influence between the warring camps of the cutter cranks and the sloop reactionaries. He was the first American to begin drafting yacht designs, and his 1879 iron sloop *Mischief* was the first scientifically-designed America's Cup defender, in the sense that she

was a designer's creation rather than a builder's. He was probably the leading designer in the brief big-schooner revival of the early 1900's. In contrast to the *Gracie*, whose form was conceived as a gleam in a paint salesman's eye, the *Katrina*'s shape was drafted according to the scientific "Archer-Hyslop wave-form" theory. Smith was also responsible for designing some of the finest and fastest big Long Island Sound passenger steamers, beginning with the famous *Richard Peck*.[80]

The replacement of the New York sloop's big single headsail with divided headsails apparently reflected the influence of the cutter. Two or three smaller headsails were much easier to manage in a breeze than was a big single sail, although it was realized that in moderate weather the single sail was faster. Coincidentally, the double-headstay rig gave more stability to the mast, and better satisfied the sloop-man's traditional preoccupation with having flat-setting sails. This particular concern dated back at least to the fifties and lasted well into the eighties, when it was finally determined that some increased draft was preferable. Cary Smith was the first to devise the roach reef, which allowed the draft of a sail to be altered according to conditions. The air-foil phenomenon, upon which the modern jib-headed rig is based, was not perceived in the nineteenth century.[81]

Stebbins copy negative 3185

A drifter off Newport

Big sloops and schooners of the New York and Eastern Yacht Clubs in a discouraging race. The white sloop, left of center, with the prominent spinnaker, looks to be the Burgess Cup defender *Puritan*; the dark schooner at the right is unmistakably the old schooner *Dauntless*. The big sloop far in the lead appears to be the *Volunteer*, Burgess' last defender, which had caught a lucky slant soon after the start.

A correspondent for the *Times* described the event:

> The truth, in brief, is that the affair was a miserable series of flukes from beginning to end, and served only to make everyone heartily sick and tired of the protracted and more or less unsuccessful cruise of the gallant New York squadron . . . The race was fifteen miles to leeward and return, and as a test of sailing ability was probably the most worthless ever sailed in American waters . . . The fleet will disband tomorrow, and then the . . . glory of the yachtsman will fade. The fleet of the New York Yacht Club will be disbanded, the yachtsman will walk about the streets and be indistinguishable from ordinary citizens, and when he is pointed out the observer will exclaim: "Great Scott is that the thing I've been admiring!" And when the excitement is over the calm mind will have an opportunity to estimate at its true worth the absurd pretensiveness and sham importance of a lot of fellows who can sit on the quarter-deck and look wise while the sailing master handles the boat. Indeed, it has been remarked by several members of the Eastern Yacht Club, who are true yachtsmen and know how to handle a boat, while they are quite as wealthy as the New York men, and generally bluer of blood, that the flagship of the New York fleet was no place for him . . . "There's too much gold lace and red tape for me," said one of them, "I can't go there."
>
> *New York Times*, August 21, 1888

Although the Easterners may not have taken themselves quite so seriously, their club rules appear to have been copied wholesale from the New York book, and contain as much nonsense about flag etiquette, crew uniforms, and fleet protocol. On an average cruise the New York squadron probably wore out as many signal halyards and exploded as much black powder as a South American naval fleet on maneuvers. Nineteenth-century Americans were greatly concerned with ceremony, costumes, and role-playing.

There were no doubt many very able yachtsmen in the New York Yacht Club, although there were probably relatively few who could make much of a showing racing against the better professional sailing masters. A major reason, certainly, was simply that the types of yachts which had developed (partly because of the availability of skilled professionals) were big, complicated, and unforgiving. They required expert handling to be maneuvered safely during a windy start. Unlike the average yachtsman, the professional sailing master of the 1880's generally had the advantage of a lifetime under sail. Paid helmsmen were an accepted part of yachting and caused no more notice than a paid jockey in a horse race.

In general, the amateur situation in the smaller classes was very much better, although even many of the so-called Corinthian races of the progressive Seawanhaka Yacht Club merely involved a restriction on the number of professionals who could be carried.[82] In general, the occasional attempts to organize crews of young amateurs to supply the beef aboard large racing yachts were considered akin to a collegiate stunt.[83] The New York Yacht Club, of course, did not have the benefit of truly small boat racing, since it had been decided that nothing less than forty feet could be considered a yacht or admitted to the club. A writer in the mid-eighties commented:

> Owners of the New York Yacht Club then [in the sixties] far more than now, were practical yachtsmen; that is, they sailed or knew how to sail their own craft. Of course, some do this even now, but the proportion of experts among the New York Yacht Club owners is not, I think, as large as among the owners in the Atlantic, or Seawanhaka, Corinthian, or the Larchmont Clubs, and to go still further down in the scale of importance, the proportion of experts, that is, men who habitually sail the yachts they own, is greater in the Jersey City, New Jersey, and Knickerbocker Yacht Clubs than in the others I have named.[84]

Stebbins copy negative 1921

The schooner yacht *Constellation*

The jib topsail comes in as the schooner yacht *Constellation* enjoys a fresh breeze on Long Island Sound. The *Constellation* was a deep center-boarder, designed by Edward Burgess, and built of iron in 1888 for E. D. Morgan of Newport. She never raced very much, but once ran from Vineyard Haven to Marblehead averaging better than thirteen knots.[85] She lived until 1941, spending most of her life at Marblehead, where she was regarded with great affection by the community.

At the time of the photograph the *Constellation* had been sold to Bayard Thayer of Boston, Mr. Morgan being more interested in his new wonder of a sloop, the *Gloriana*. Mr. Thayer was of an old merchant shipping family, and apparently earned enough money at birth to devote his remaining years to the pursuits of arboriculture, sailing, hunting, and the breeding of wily game birds and fast horses.

Mr. Thayer's sailing master was Captain Nate Watson, one of the best-known and most respected professionals on the coast. Watson was a native of Clark's Island, Plymouth, where his family had lived since before 1700. Before taking up yachting, he had been a fisherman and had modeled and built some very fine boats and small yachts. He was a skilled helmsman, and in the years when the schooner was not placed in commission he sailed some noted racing yachts.[86]

The crew of the *Constellation* came from a small village in Norway. They arrived in May, and went home in October, after the schooner had been laid up in Beverly. Nate Watson's relationship to his sailors was as father to sons, and the yacht was superbly managed. She was routinely sailed to her berth in crowded, constricted Marblehead Harbor.

The chances are very good that the man at the wheel, sighting forward along the lee rail, is Nate Watson.

Stebbins plate 4419 (detail)

The Hanley-built cat *Mucilage*

An entrancing study in the singular shape of a big Cape-style racing catboat. The conflict between the hefty rig, stepped right in the eyes, and the stable, beamy hull caused some elderly cats to become rather supple forward. We can readily appreciate how well-suited the *Mucilage's* more conservatively-rigged working cousins would be for fishing in the shoal, choppy waters off the Cape.

The *Mucilage's* mainsail (in 1907) was about a handkerchief short of one thousand feet in area. Her boom was just under thirty feet in length (the *Mucilage* herself being twenty-six feet, six inches on the waterline), and her bowsprit was nearly sixteen feet long. The long spar draped over the cabin top is the spinnaker pole, and it was probably jointed for disassembly and normal stowage. What a racing cat's spinnaker lacked in hoist it made up for in width. Despite the fact that no jib is set, the *Mucilage* appears to be carrying no weather helm.

The *Mucilage* was built in 1887 by Charley Hanley for his own use. She gained a reputation for speed, and in 1888 was bought by E. D. Morgan of Newport. There were apparently several very fast cats at Newport, and the locals thought their champion was close to being the ultimate catboat. Entered in the Fourth of July regatta, the *Mucilage* finished thirty minutes ahead of the nearest Narragansett flash, and peace and quiet were restored to the Bay. Having served Mr. Morgan's ends, the *Mucilage* was soon sold to Elbridge Gerry for use by one of his sons when vacationing at the family's Newport cottage. The big cat may have proven more than a handful for the young gentleman, as she spent most of the next sixteen years locked up in a boathouse, and eventually was all but forgotten.

In the meantime, the popularity of catboat racing diminished greatly. Racing cats were roundly condemned by yachting reformers as extreme and dangerous anachronisms, and younger sailors fell for the charms of freakish "skows" and miserable Sondor Klasse boats, as well as for the many local restricted-design classes. By the early 1900's there remained but a few active fleets of racing catboats, kept in service by an insular band of middle-aged old-time catboat die-hards. The fleet of the Quincy Yacht Club was the best, and contained many of the legendary old brutes of the catboat's glory days. In 1906, chasing a rumor, Commodore Frank Crane discovered the old *Mucilage* in her boathouse, bought her, and brought her to Quincy. There, renamed the *Iris*, she was the 1907 champion.[87] A guest described racing aboard the *Iris* in a breeze:

On the floor of the cockpit sat the mainsheet man . . . A braw lad was he, youngest of the crew, being only thirty-five or thereabouts. He tipped the scales at 250 pounds, and looked as he sat on the floor of the cockpit, his feet braced, grimly holding a turn around the mainsheet cleat on the floor, as if most of it were bone and sinew.

The others tailed on; around the [mark] barrel went *Iris* with a sharp luff; quickly the sheet came in, and quickly also over the lee rail came a couple of barrels or so of water. When a boat of 12-foot breadth dips up the brine thus freely under four reefs, you may believe there is snap and weight to the breeze . . . The Commodore was sailing her as nearly on edge as he had ever done. A fine sight it was to see the veteran of thirty racing seasons thus skillfully balancing his boat . . . It spoke of long and patient practice with a type which few men learn to sail properly. No "lead mine" slung low in a thin keel was on this boat to keep her on her feet. Her stability was due solely to breadth and a delicate touch on the helm . . . [88]

Racing cats did carry ballast in the bilges — the *Iris* had two tons of copper dross — and they sank quickly if filled. Nevertheless, they had great style, and even so progressive a designer as Professor George Owen, one of the fathers of the Universal Measurement Rule, was moved to reflect: "Yet with all her defects the typical racing 'cat' possessed a certain grandeur, and noble were many traditions connected with her career. Her memory will long outlive many of her successors."[89]

Incidentally, another Hanley creation of the *Mucilage's* generation, the cat-like sloop *Ramona*, is reputed to be still afloat, as a Florida houseboat. The *Ramona*, a great homely ark of a vessel, was sequestered in a boathouse at Onset from 1908 to 1946, when she emerged perfectly preserved. She was said then to be a first-class job of work, with elm frames and screw fastenings. She was subsequently twice cruised to Florida.[90]

Stebbins copy negative 1903

The excursion steamer *Taurus*

October 7, 1893

The "Iron Steamboat" *Taurus* rolls to her guards in a queasy swell off Sandy Hook as her shockingly crowded passengers try to keep their minds occupied by the America's Cup race — no simple task. At the beginning of the series between Lord Dunraven's *Valkyrie* and the American *Vigilant* the large spectator fleet made a great nuisance of itself. Steamers crowded the start, blocked the wind, and chased noisily around the course, bothering the racers with their wakes. Captain Cranfield of the *Valkyrie* complained that at times he was unable to pick out the turning mark from the confused backdrop of vessels which had steamed ahead and gathered in wait for him. Officers of the New York Yacht Club darkly predicted that future series would have to be held off Newport, comfortably removed from the thundering herd.

In fact, on most race days the spectator fleet was the best part of the show. The yachts of the Vanderbilts and the Astors rolled gunwale to gunwale with scruffy dollar-a-head boats and a tug crowded with celebrating Irish policemen. Organizations and individuals of means or refinement reserved accommodations aboard the big Long Island Sound and ocean-going coastal steamers; the man off the street crowded aboard the common excursion steamers like the *Taurus*, which he normally rode to Coney Island and Rockaway to escape the city heat.

Certainly the best racing of the event occurred after the sailing yachts had completed their performance for the day, and the huge fleet was headed for home. Here was the ideal chance to settle old arguments and start some new ones. The competition between the big Sound flyer *Richard Peck* and the Jersey Shore steamer *Monmouth* was the feature event; the side-wheel class was paced by the flashing *Republic*, up from Philadelphia, of all places.

In a story entitled "A Stupid Day on the Water," concerning the cancelled race on October 11, a *Times* reporter observed:

> Possibly the reduction of prices for accommodations all along the line had something to do with the increase in the numbers who went out to see what was generally expected to be the last of the series of races for the America's cup. Some of the excursion boats, notably the *General Slocum, Grand Republic*, and a couple of the Iron Steamboats, seemed to have dangerously large crowds aboard, and certainly close up to their licensed carrying capacity.
>
> From the deck of the *Richard Peck*, "the Queen of the Sound," as this fast and beautiful steamer is very appropriately styled, these crowded boats looked like a huckleberry bush overloaded with ripe fruit, or like hives about which too many bees to fill them had tried to swarm.

Stebbins plate 4631

The widespread interest among common citizens in both Britain and America concerning the America's Cup races is curious. No doubt even the majority of the witnesses would have been hard-pressed to distinguish a catboat from a coal schooner. Certainly strong nationalistic feelings were aroused, but such emotions are often themselves symptoms. It seems likely that the races provided some welcome diversion from the very real difficulties of life at a time when there were few major sporting events or other mass entertainment. The "Gay Nineties" was a confused period of great social inequities, when ordinary people tried to reconcile their faith in progress with the contradictory realities of stubborn financial depression. What could be more oddly intriguing than to spend a day on a steamer gazing down upon the truly wealthy on their yachts, and then to return to the headline, datelined London:

Starving Miners Have Work

To Be Taken Back at the Old Wage

Advances of Money Will Be Made to
Relieve the Pressing Needs of Families . . .
The Men Will Consent to a Ten Per Cent
Reduction in December . . .
The Greatest Strike in History
Seems Near its End

New York Times, October 12, 1893

Such contrasts appear with some frequency in the newspapers of the era. For example, the yachtsmen out exercising their sloops and catboats in the frontispiece photograph of Hingham Bay are hopefully not so insulated by class differences as to prevent them from feeling anger and compassion for the previous day's events at Lattimer, Pennsylvania. There, sixty unarmed Hungarian coal miners had been shot down by sheriff's deputies. Many were shot in the back, and the correspondent for the *Transcript* reported that a single warning shot would have served to disperse the orderly gathering.[91]

This is not to imply that the yachtsmen should be feeling guilty about spending a lovely, crisp, early-autumn day out sailing. Life, of course, is not that simple. We know from our own imperfect times that in such tragedies everyone is partly to blame — in this instance, everyone used coal — and yet, no *one* is to blame. Taken singly, even the cowardly

deputies would probably emerge as distressingly ordinary people, reacting from fear, stupidity, and panic, created by an environment of prejudice.

It does seem, however, that the more comfortable classes of Americans, such as the boat-owning Bostonians, were conveniently shielded from having to feel great concern over social injustice occurring in distant places by the lingering regionalism of the recent pre-industrial past. The *Transcript* might well print a full column concerned with a local yacht race, yet would have only the barest description, often several days dated, of the lynching of an innocent man in Missouri. The inference clearly was that, as regrettable as it might be, this sorry business was the affair of the people of Missouri. Today, with distance and regionalism all but overcome by technology, Missouri would be answerable to an aroused nation.

Both the charming and civilized scene at Hingham Bay and the barbarism of the coal fields were by-products of nineteenth-century industrialism. The yachts, and the summer cottages situated on the developed Hull drumlin rising in the background, were owned by the Silas Laphams of the business world. Hull, in a sense, was the post–Civil War counterpart to the exclusive peninsula of Nahant, the seaside resort of Boston's older mercantile families (some of whom then undoubtedly held interests in the coal industry), where the comparison would not have been appreciated. Hull's Nantasket Beach was the tacky summer magnet for the excursion crowd from Boston and the industrial hinterlands. In the nineties the corrupt town fathers of Hull grew fat feeding off the common vices of the common man.[92]

Stebbins plate 4631 detail)

The sloop *Columbia* dismasted

1899

The future Cup defender *Columbia*, designed and built by the Herreshoffs, freshly dismasted off Newport. The ruined mast was an experimental steel model, and collapsed due to a faulty stay. The sailors — who are Norwegians and former Deer Isle fishermen — are busy gathering up sails and rigging so that the *Columbia* may be towed back to the Herreshoff plant at Bristol, where her old wooden mast will be restepped. The big coastal tug *Waltham*, apparently under charter to the selection committee, and a white steam yacht stand by.

Before getting into the Cup defender business, Nat Herreshoff and his brother John, who was blind, had spent many years designing and building advanced steam engines and launches. Their very complete manufacturing facility, which included a major sail loft, gave them complete control over every stage of construction, and permitted them the fullest opportunity for experimentation. New spars, sails, and fittings could be turned out quickly and well. Both of the Herreshoffs were gifted craftsmen working wood and metal, and they employed some of the most highly skilled artisans in the world.[93]

The brothers were an extremely inventive and resourceful team. In the seventies they built several very successful catamarans, which featured articulating hulls with ball and socket joints. In the nineties Nat clearly emerged as the outstanding racing yacht designer in the world. He designed all aspects of his vessels and was responsible for many inventions, including the cross-cut sail. The Herreshoff specialty was light construction of great strength.

Nat was also a skilled helmsman, and is credited with devising the tactic of downwind tacking. He commanded the *Vigilant* in her famous heavy-weather race against the *Valkyrie II*, which he may have won with the idea of shaking out the reefed mainsail while running before the wind. This was accomplished by slinging a sailor from a gantline, and hauling him along the boom with an outhaul while he cut the reef points.

It is a relief to discover that Nat was also very human. It must be said that many of his steamers (typified by his personal yacht *Roamer*) and some of his sailers were extremely homely in appearance. He was obsessed by secretiveness, and the Bristol plant was operated under strict security measures which other designers thought childish. The Cup sloop *Colonia* was allegedly designed too shoal because he didn't want to have to pay to dredge his launching slip. She was, allegedly, not fitted with a centerboard because Oliver Iselin had contracted for a second sloop — the *Vigilant* — which was guaranteed to be able to outsail the *Colonia*. The Herreshoffs were never again permitted to build two Cup defenders at the same time. Many of Nat's customers appear to have held "the Wizard" in greater professional respect than personal affection.[94]

Skipper Charlie Barr, with his arms crossed, stands abaft the wheel talking with designer-builder Nat Herreshoff. The small gathering behind them presumably includes the manager and part owner, Oliver Iselin, and others connected with the principal owner, J. P. Morgan. The sails of the other candidate, the older sloop *Defender*, appear in the distance beyond the steam yacht.

The practice of substituting true Maine Yankees for the usual Scandinavian "whitewashed" variety was begun by Mr. Iselin aboard the *Defender* in 1895. It was a gesture quite in keeping with the nationalistic and racial concerns of the times. A majority of Deer Isle men were signed aboard the *Columbia*, in part to counter public criticism of the employment of Charlie Barr, who had only recently taken out citizenship papers. The fishermen had done well aboard the *Defender*, where they got along well with old Captain Henry Haff, but aboard the *Columbia* there was some friction. For the 1901 trials Barr insisted on signing a Norwegian crew. Deer Islanders were recruited for the new candidate *Constitution*, and were among the parties blamed for her poor performance against the *Columbia*. Charlie Barr explained that he preferred a Scandinavian crew over the independent Deer Islanders because they would obey an order at once, without first considering its merits.[95]

Stebbins copy negative 10240 (detail)

The Victory Float, New York

September 1899

The Victory Float in the spectacular naval parade which welcomed Admiral Dewey home from his conquests. Protocol demanded that the procession extend up the Hudson to Grant's Tomb, so that "the great warrior who sleeps within" might be apprised of the situation. The river bank is thick with the assembled multitude, and there are no hotel rooms to be had in the city.

It was fortunate that the wind was slight during the parade, for the sake of the pilots of the unwieldy excursion steamers, and for the sake of the floating statuary. A day or so before the parade the seventy-eight-foot-high masterwork was involved in a collision with a tug, and the damage is still very apparent. Despite the emergency shoring, the distressed sculptor expressed fear that if the wind blew in excess of three or four knots Victory would come tumbling down.

The Dewey celebration was perhaps the symbolic high-water mark of America's career as a nineteenth-century imperialist power. The great plaster-of-Paris Victory Arch hurriedly erected in Madison Square would have made Caesar feel right at home. The press exulted in self-satisfaction over the wonderful war it had produced, and promised the nation a great future in the Far East. A writer for the *Herald* felt compelled to remind his readers that even on this day of triumph the tireless reporters, like the stokers on the steamers, remained hard at their work.

If the most interesting historical periods are those which involve the greatest contradictions, then the late nineteenth century in America must be considered nearly as fascinating a time as the present. For example, the plaster absurdity on the barge stands in glaring contrast to the spare and stylish tugs, which represented the very best tradition of good nineteenth-century functional design.

The steamer in the foreground is apparently the Long Island Sound steamer *Middletown*, normally operated between New York and Hartford.

Stebbins copy negative 10447

Aboard the steam yacht *Formosa*

The "dining room" of the steam yacht *Formosa*, a 133-foot (waterline) steel vessel built by the Atlantic Works, East Boston. The owner, George Fabyan, was interested in New England textiles. A woman, perhaps the lady of the yacht, is partially reflected in the mirror of the sideboard.

Stebbins photographs show the interiors of most yachts finished in oppressively dark paneling, in contrast to the sunlit expanses of deck. Many cry out for some free application of white paint, which would have served to display the fine joinery to better advantage. The *Formosa*'s interior is finished with relative simplicity and taste; many yacht cabins were embellished with bushels of carved specimens of marine fauna, flora, and flotsam, and vast lengths of wooden "rope" molding. Such treatments usually reflected the owners' wishes; often the most difficult part of a designer's job was to arrive diplomatically at a practical and tasteful interior. In 1903 a naval architect wrote:

> It would be easy to name many costly yachts, built within the past few dozen years, which proved complete failures, the prime cause being that the owner did not realize the differences between a yacht which must float within some definite limit of displacement, and a house on solid land, with a driveway by which coal, ice and provisions may be delivered at all times.[96]

Many steam yacht owners did not discover their overpowering love for the sea until after they found themselves with great quantities of money to pour into it. (And even then it is likely that few developed much affection for the bounding main as such, considering the roll characteristics of most steamers.) The production of American millionaires was greatly stepped up around the turn of the century, thanks to high tariffs, the formation of hosts of trusts and combinations, and other enriching restraints of trade. This situation led to a great increase in the market for steam yachts, which had become major status symbols, particularly around New York. There were, after all, few sporting outlets open to a middle-aged titan of industry commensurate with his position in life. Those afflicted with truly serious wealth often had to work harder to spend than to acquire, and a properly conceived steam yacht could convince even the flushest financier that he was enjoying his leisure time to the fullest extent.

The costs of building and maintaining a steam yacht varied greatly. The simple costs of crew wages, coal, and basic maintenance were not considered excessive — a yacht owner in the eighties estimated that the basic annual expenses for a yacht roughly the *Formosa*'s size, kept in commission for the summer only, would run from twelve to fifteen thousand dollars.[97] The crunch came with the associated expenses of entertaining. It was said that during the two-week cruise of the New York Yacht Squadron, Commodore Gerry, aboard his 300-ton steamer *Electra*, spent more for champagne than for coal, crew wages, and keep.[98] James Gordon Bennett was said in the eighties to spend $150,000 a year for the use of his steamer *Namouna*.[99] Not surprisingly, the number of steamers which were put into commission every spring at City Island and South Brooklyn yacht basins was said to be a sensitive economic barometer.[100]

The formation of the Steel Trust in about 1900 led to the construction of many large steamers. Clinton Crane, who designed several of these yachts, has written about two westerners who got rich selling tin plate to the trust, and who then decided to enter New York society aboard two big steamers built from the same design. One owner insisted on so many interior additions and alterations that his yacht floated far below her marks, fully half-sunk. The other gentleman once became quite cross over the manner in which the main saloon dining table had been laid. To communicate his displeasure, he gave a tremendous tug on the damask table cloth, sending crystal, china, and silverware crashing to the floor. Then, driving the point home, he picked the steward up by the back of the neck and the seat of his pants and pitched him overboard. The yacht was anchored in Oyster Bay at the time, and the flying steward narrowly missed crash-landing into the launch which was arriving alongside with the dinner guests.[101]

Stebbins copy negative 5060

The "thirty-footer" *Saracen*

The "thirty-footer" *Saracen* of Marblehead in a race in New York Bay. The *Saracen* was a typical Burgess-Lawley creation, termed either a cutter or a sloop, or a cutter-like sloop.

The increased intercourse between yachtsmen of Boston and New York reflected the growing commercial and social contacts between businessmen of the two regions, and the success of the Burgess Cup defenders. The relations between the New York and Eastern Yacht Clubs had been very close for many years.

Although the *Saracen* is beating to windward with her topmast housed, and is showing no light canvas, it is apparent that the thirties did not suffer from a lack of sail. C. F. Adams recalled sailing the "forty-footer" *Papoose*, which, while larger, was otherwise quite similar:

> In shape the *Papoose* was very good. The rig, however, was large and difficult, with a long bowsprit which would tuck itself under every considerable sea and come up again with sore complaint; a boom far over the stern and quite horrid when reefing was necessary, a big club-topsail which could not then be left up, and often would not come down without taking charge of everything; and a topmast which had to be housed whenever it blew hard. Then your friends needed web feet.[102]

Under the New York Yacht Club's version of the Seawanhaka Rule, length was taxed more heavily than was sail area, and designers discovered that the rule effectively made sail area the greater factor in determining speed. Accordingly, large and unhandy sail plans were devised which served to give an advantage to the young, the rich, and the foolhardy. W. P. Stephens, a "reformer," wrote in the nineties:

> We find that any class, however popular at first, under the general measurement rule and existing classification, but without special restrictions, has a life of one or possibly two years. This has been the case of the forties, the thirties, the forty-six footers and the Boston twenty-one footers. The reaction caused by the lapsing of a class does incalculable harm to yachting, driving men into steam or into other sports . . .[103]

In 1889 the club established a special committee to re-evaluate the measurement situation. The committee's report indicated that there was no great problem:

> In a class of small vessels like that of forty feet, a class unknown to

this Club previous to last season, any extravagance of rig or proportion may be of little moment, and a sailing machine costing no more than one of those may to a person able to afford it be regarded as a harmless and even interesting means of amusement.[104]

The club did make some rule changes. A technicality which had encouraged long gaffs was changed, and an attempt was made to place the factors of sail area and length on equal footing. The unforeseen result of this reversion to the original Seawanhaka Rule was to allow the two factors to be traded off against each other, which only made the situation worse.[105]

One direct effect of the confused measurement situation was the establishment of numerous local restricted and one-design classes. The first restricted class was the twenty-one-foot knockabout class developed in Massachusetts. These were modestly-rigged sloops without bowsprits which could be sailed in safety and comfort by middle-aged men, and were good either for racing or simply "knocking about." The prototype made a very great impression sailing among the spectator fleet at the 1892 Fishermen's Race, which was held in a gale of wind.

While the move towards restricted classes is easily understood, we should not overlook the many advances made by open-class racing. For those who could afford to build a new boat every year, open-class racing provided a year-round sport with a winter warmed by anticipation.

Incidentally, later in the season the *Saracen* would be one of the two thirties humiliated by the catboat *Harbinger*. In fairness, however, it should be said that subsequent contests showed that the *Harbinger* could not always have it her way.

The dark form of the big coasting schooner off to leeward is an indication of how very much more interesting the coastal waters were then. The great array of coastal shipping must have added much pleasure to everyday yachting.

Stebbins copy negative 2425

Another view of the Dewey Day parade

Stebbins apparently had the foresight to buy a ticket on one of the highest steamers on the river. There were moments of confusion in the parade, reportedly caused by the recklessness of some of the smaller excursion vessels. Here, the *Glen* is backing down, probably to the consternation of the *Twilight*, astern. Beyond the *Twilight* we see the old-style Hudson River night-boat *City of Troy*, with her large paddle-boxes, and boilers mounted outboard on the overhanging guards. The old steamer with the twin stacks at the left of the photo is the *Rosedale*, for thirty years the special pride of the city of Bridgeport. By way of contrast, she is close aboard the modern propeller steamer *Middletown*.

The nearly simultaneous scheduling of the Dewey Day parade and the *Columbia-Shamrock* Cup races created a tremendous demand for excursion craft. Months in advance speculators were busy hiring all the available tonnage, creating a new trading commodity. As the great day drew near, the steamboat inspectors worked overtime licensing tugs and lighters, and steamers began to arrive from points all along the seaboard.

Dewey! Dewey! Dewey! Were it not for the name a visiting backwoods hermit would have been excused for thinking that the Second Coming had commenced. At the height of the mania the newspapers no longer permitted people to simply die; rather, "Excitement Caused Death," or the deceased was "Stricken while Raising a Flag." Displaying commendable zeal, several of the plasterers frantically trying to finish the great Madison Square Victory Arch died at their trowels.

Chicago, Ill., Sept. 29.— An Indian, Henry Little Bear; Henry Welch, an Irishman, and Oliver Schwarzmeister, a German, became acquainted Thursday last, and all three have to appear in a police court Wednesday as the result.

The row began over a discussion about how long it would take Dewey to blow up the entire German fleet. Little Bear held it would require about an hour for the operation, while Welch declared that ten minutes would be ample time. Schwarzmeister thought Dewey couldn't do it in less than thirty years. The Indian and the Irishman began fighting, and the contest was so intense that the German turned in a fire alarm. The police arrested all three.

New York Times, September 30, 1899

Stebbins plate 10452

Herreshoff's mighty *Reliance*

The Cup defender *Reliance* smokes past the Brenton Reef light vessel in a pre-trials race. The *Constitution* and the *Columbia* were the other, older candidates.

The *Reliance* was the biggest and probably the fastest of all of the Cup yachts, and was the last to be designed under the bedeviled Seawanhaka Rule. Clinton Crane, an eminent authority, believed that the *Reliance* could even have beaten the modern 1937 J-boat *Ranger* going to windward, boat for boat.

> . . . I can remember very well watching *Reliance* racing *Columbia* off Newport in August, 1903 . . . *Columbia* got the best of the start and was standing in toward the Narragansett shore. *Reliance* came up from astern, bore away, sailed through *Columbia*'s lee, then walked up right across her bow. It was a sight to be remembered.[106]

Nat Herreshoff had immediately seen the loophole implicit in the 1890 rule, and designed the 1891 forty-six-footer *Gloriana* with a severely cutaway forefoot, which allowed her to carry more sail. The logical path, which was followed progressively through all the Cup yachts of the nineties, led to the extreme overhangs of the *Reliance*. Designers saw the rule as a challenge to increase sail area and sail-carrying power while limiting waterline length. A "shovel-nosed" or "snout-bowed" rule cheater such as the *Reliance* actually gained length, and power, as she heeled; she measured ninety feet on the waterline when floating upright, but when heeled sailed on 112 feet. She was 144 feet on deck, while her rig extended over 200 feet in length. No one claimed that such models represented a wholesome or desirable type of yacht; in particular, the long ends often pounded heavily. But they were very fast under the rule. When the rule was written the waterline lengths and sail areas of large yachts were in healthy proportion, and the technological advances which would make possible huge sail plans on even the largest yachts were simply not foreseen.

The *Reliance* was a typically magnificent Herreshoff engineering accomplishment. She was constructed with the Herreshoffs' ingenious longitudinal framing system, which combined lightness with great strength, and permitted her bronze hull plates to be fitted flush. She carried a measured sail area of 16,200 square feet, all hung from a single mast, which was itself a notable structure. Her gigantic mainsail was cut from specially-woven No. 000 hard duck; by contrast, the sails for a six-masted schooner were cut from No. 00 duck. The topmast was housed inside the steel lowermast, its heel coming to rest just below the waterline. The topmast rigging was left behind and picked up again automatically, requiring no sailors aloft. The rudder was hollow, and could be trimmed by water ballast, which was regulated with a foot-operated air pump. Advanced two-speed winches with multiple-disk clutches were mounted below deck and gave her great quickness when maneuvering. Foot brakes allowed little Charlie Barr to steer the huge sloop through a long, hard race without relief.[107]

Also typically, this wonderful and costly machine was intended and used for but a single summer's sport.

Stebbins' photograph shows the *Reliance* sailing under optimal conditions, with little sea, and with the wind almost more than enough. The big Cup freaks were designed for the average light summer racing conditions, and carrying-on in a strong breeze meant stretched sails, or worse. Earlier in the month the three contenders had unwisely been raced in heavy, three-lowers weather, and the *Constitution* had broken her gaff, while the *Columbia* lost several sailors overboard, one of whom drowned. Of course, the apparent wind experienced by a big racing machine being driven to weather was of greater velocity and from farther ahead than the actual wind which was blowing.

In the race photographed here, the *Constitution* lost her topmast, and later in the day, while jibing, the *Reliance*'s steel gaff collapsed. Some idea of the proportions of the *Reliance*'s rig may be realized from the fact that this gaff measured fully seventy feet long, or as long as the mainboom of a good-sized Gloucester fishing schooner. That she was campaigned even one summer with no other significant accident is equally remarkable.

Stebbins plate 14515

Having seen the *Reliance* out of water for the first time and not
having seen her in, I have no hesitancy in saying that she is an
overgrown, ugly brute, but over and beyond that she is a splendid
conception, splendidly carried out. One cannot but admire Herreshoff's courage in daring to take the step he has. It shows more
plainly than ever what a consummate master he is of the engineer's
art.

T. F. Day[108]

In addition to her Scotch-born skipper, Charlie Barr, the *Reliance*
was manned by a Scandinavian (predominantly Norwegian) crew including two mates, a boatswain, a carpenter, a rigger, two sailmakers, three
quartermasters, and fifty sailors.

As might be expected, the trend toward long overhangs was taken
up with enthusiasim in the smaller classes, where rule-cheating had
become a favorite wintertime activity. The most extreme examples were
the freakish "skows," of which some were actually twice as long overall as
on the waterline. The sloop *Outlook*, which was designed by Starling
Burgess (Edward Burgess' son) to defend the Quincy Cup in 1902, was
twenty-one feet on the waterline, and fifty-one feet overall. Constructed
with a complicated arrangement of steel girders, she and others of her
persuasion might better be classified as "stunts." They are very ade-
quately represented by photographs in the Stebbins Collection.

The blatant loopholes of the Seawanhaka Rule were finally closed
by the so-called Herreshoff Rule, adopted by the New York Yacht Club in
1903. Devised by the great rule-cheater himself, this measure introduced displacement into the equation, thereby eliminating the freak
skows, and measured the length from one-half the distance from the
centerline, thus taxing shovel-like bows prohibitively, and discouraging
excessive sail area. The rule was not without its own defects, although
these were reduced by modifications in 1905, resulting in the so-called
Universal Rule, which was widely adopted and remained in effect for
nearly thirty years.[109]

Stebbins plate 14515 (detail)

The infamous steamer *General Slocum*

The New York Harbor excursion steamer *General Slocum* at the Cup races presents a gay picture shadowed by grim foreboding. There is an indication that Stebbins realized as much, for on several occasions he took photographs of densely-packed excursion steamers. As the *Times* would belatedly editorialize on June 16, 1904:

> Whenever there is a pageant upon the water, in the form of a civic celebration or of an international yacht race, there are always to be seen in it half a dozen of these antiquated craft, loaded to the guards with humanity of which every one excites, in the passengers of safer steamers and even in her own, the reflection of how helpless she would be and how hopeless those on board, if the long expected should happen.

On the previous day the *Slocum* was in the East River bound out for Hell Gate with a large crowd of women and children, members of a German parish group on an annual picnic. The steamer caught fire forward, and the flames spread rapidly through the newly-painted and tinder-dry wooden superstructure. Grievously, the captain elected to continue on course at full speed against a fresh wind, heading for a cove on North Brother Island, rather than steering directly for the nearby shore or heading downwind. The fire quickly enveloped the vessel, burning to death hundreds who were trapped under the collapsing decks, and driving hundreds overboard, where most drowned. Over nine hundred persons died, many in the most horrible manner conceivable. And the suffering did not end there, for many fathers returned home from work to discover that all in their families were dead.

The subsequent investigations and hearings revealed many interesting aspects of the excursion business, and raised serious questions as to the competence or loyalties of the government steamboat inspectors. It was disclosed, among other things, that many of the lifejackets were useless, the fire apparatus was largely defective, and the crew was totally untrained for such an emergency.

The *Slocum* had long possessed a reputation as an unlucky vessel, or worse, and had been involved in numerous groundings, collisions, and incidents. On many occasions her owners had been cited for overloading beyond the steamer's licensed capacity of 2500. Once in 1894, while bound up from Rockaway in the dark with a crowd estimated at 4700, she went aground and lost her electrical lighting. In the ensuing panic many were injured.

On occasion, it would seem, the captain of a New York Harbor excursion craft faced perils more reminiscent of service in the South China Sea. In 1900 the *Slocum* was chartered to take 900 "Paterson Anarchists" from Jersey City to Rockaway. Outside Sandy Hook a sea had built up, and a delegation of the passengers requested that the steamer turn around. When the captain refused, an angry mob attempted to seize the pilot house, where they were met by the deckhands and the spare men from the engine room. A pitched battle followed, which was decided when the crew was finally able to back the Jerseyites into the cabins and lock the doors.

Stebbins plate 4678

T Wharf, Boston

January 1902

A wonderful photograph of a most interesting place. With the exception of the "sloop boat" in the right foreground and the two little "schooner boats" at the far left, all of the vessels lying alongside are fishing schooners. Down the way we see two bowsprits jutting over the caplog, while the tiny T Wharf tug is at work in the dock, trying either to extract a departing schooner, or to make room for a new arrival. The outboard schooner in the second tier has not been in long, and her bulwarks are still white with ice. Bowsprits, overhanging mainbooms, and independently-minded fishermen were the curses of the wharf tug's life. The square floats in the left foreground are lobster cars.

T Wharf was always jammed with fish, fishermen, fish buyers, and fish cutters. Although groundfish were landed the year around, mid-winter marked the height of the large haddock fishery. In summer the great cry was for mackerel, and crack Gloucester seiners crowded the docks.

Offshore lay wonderful fishing grounds, which in 1902 could be expected to supply an unending abundance of good food. Modern technology combined with age-old greed and short-sightedness has now all but looted these incalculably valuable natural treasuries.

At the turn of the century Boston was the leading fresh fish market in the country. The fresh fish business resulted from improved cold storage and transportation facilities which made it possible to ship iced fish long distances. It was made feasible on the fishing grounds by the adoption of dory trawling and purse seining, which made it possible for the fishermen to catch large fares within a short time. The business was closely tied to the development of fast schooners.

The bigger schooner in the foreground is probably a regular offshore trawler, a frequenter of Browns and Georges Banks. She carries long-stocked banks anchors and fiber-cable, which could be cut with an axe in an emergency. Unlike many of the other schooners, she has left her main topmast stopped for the winter. Vessels which fished the offshore banks in the winter had to be able to take care of themselves, since tide-torn Georges is famous country for easterly gales, and the passage home was subject to powerful and bitter westerly winds. In 1902 ten vessels and eighty-two fishermen were drowned from the New England vessel fleet.[110]

The small schooner to the left, the *Estelle* S. *Nunan* of Gloucester, is probably employed in the "shore fishery," as is the sloop. The shore fishermen worked the numerous smaller grounds nearer the coast, fishing

lighter gear in shoaler water with one man to a dory. They ranged occasionally out to Browns and Cashes, and down to South Shoals. (The sloop has a duck boat sitting in one of her nested dories, and so, for all I know, she may land a few mergansers along with her haddock and cod.)

Small schooners very similar to the *Nunan* were owned and manned out of small Maine ports with local crews; by this date the bigger offshore vessels sailing from Boston and Gloucester were manned largely by Nova Scotians, Irish, Portuguese, and Newfoundlanders.

Charley York, a boy from Bailey Island, Casco Bay, made his first trip aboard a Maine shore schooner in March 1902, not very long after Stebbins took this photograph.

We left Water Cove for the Sou' Sou' West Grounds off Monhegan in the *Eva And Mildred* with a crew of ten fishermen and a cook; father was the skipper . . . Father made it just as tough for me as he could and I was called on to do everything the older men did. We had breakfast before daylight, was put off in our dories at sunrise to set trawl, was picked up for dinner, and then dropped off to haul.

Two or three miles of trawl with a good catch of fish on it comes in hard for a 15-year old boy. Each man was back on board with his catch by the middle of the afternoon, had supper, and then dressed out the fish. When that was done, we baited trawl for the next day . . . With a full fare we made a 24-hour run to T wharf in Boston, sold our catch, and shared $27.10 apiece. That was big money in them times for four days of fishin'. When everything was shipshape on board, the men invited me to go uptown with 'em to a beer parlor.

With money in my pocket and a bunch of friends, I never felt bigger in my life and I was all set for the next trip.[111]

Fish dealers hired Stebbins to take a number of T Wharf views, and several have survived. To try to imagine what this scene would be like without the schooners, the fish, and the various fish people demonstrates the hopeless task facing developers who think they can "recreate" the atmosphere along an old waterfront which no longer supports productive economic activity. Slips filled by plastic yachts and even a floating relic or two will not suffice.

Stebbins copy negative 13037

The *Erl King* at the Cup trials

"English" steam yachts (so-called, although most were products of Scotland) were owned by the most discriminating American steam yachtsmen. The *Erl King*, built at Leith from designs by St. Claire Byrne, was later bought by a Poughkeepsie "businessman." By common agreement the handsomest English steamers were designed by the renowned George Watson. As a group, the English steamers were slower than American yachts (they were rather over-built to Lloyd's rules, and fitted with heavy Scotch marine boilers) but in beauty of form, thoroughness of engineering, and quality of detail finish they were the standard of perfection. They were modeled after the lovely Scotish sailing clippers.

> It is the proper caper for those who can afford it nowadays to have an English steam yacht, and to be thoroughly English they must burn soft coal. It was noticed that the *May, White Layde, Conquerer,* and *Ituna* all burned soft coal [on the cruise] and made the atmosphere very smoky.
> *New York Times,* August 8, 1893

Incidentally, the *May,* a handsome Watson steamer owned by Commodore E. D. Morgan, was cruising with a cow signed aboard to provide the guests with fresh, safe milk.[112]

High society's great interest in yacht racing in these years may be explained in part by the fact that watching the races was the primary diversion provided for the many guests aboard the steam yachts while they rested between meals. Ordinarily, watching yachts race is about as exciting as watching sheep eat grass. Clinton Crane was aboard the *May* to observe the 1903 Cup trials, and overheard several of the other guests mistaking a four-masted schooner for the seven-masted *Thomas W. Lawson.*[113]

L. Francis Herreshoff (Nat's son) was a great admirer of the big steam yachts of his youth.

> One of the things I remember about the large steam yachts was their characteristic and delightful odor. If you passed under the stern or close to leeward of one of them you smelled the combined odor of new varnish, linseed oil, brass polish, Havana cigars and champagne, all mingled with engine room smells and the slight odor of teak and other exotic woods, to say nothing of the burned gases of the naphtha launches.[114]

The naphtha launch was the first motorboat which did not have to be operated by a licensed steam engineer. Most were fitted with a little three-cylinder engine driven by the vapor of heated naphtha, which was similar in volatility to gasoline. Fewer exploded than the nature of the arrangement would seem to indicate.

Herreshoff recalled that most of the captains of the steam yachts were deep-water men who had served their time in square-riggers, and who made a good appearance. Many were English or Scots. The engineers, of course, were Scotsmen. True to legend, they were rarely separated from their beloved machinery, with but an occasional pilgrimage ashore to "destroy as much Highland Dew as possible" in company with a fellow chief. The *Erl King* had a crew of twenty-seven.[115]

A small American steam yacht is to the right; the big iron tug *Joanna* is to the left. Tugs were regularly chartered to cover yachting events. In Cup years fully half a dozen would join the cruise. Towing was a very competitive business, rates were low, and a tug could be chartered for a reasonable fee, especially as little coal would be burned. A tug made a good committee boat, and could easily assist a disabled yacht. Probably most of Stebbins' racing photos were taken from atop tugs he chartered along with fellow club members, or from committee tugs.

> The big cup defenders and schooners bowed gracefully to the rollers, the smaller boats bobbed up and down, and the steam yachts rolled as only steam yachts can. As for the tugs — well, everybody who has been aboard one in a seaway knows that they can beat anything afloat for rolling and throwing spray.
> *New York Times,* August 12, 1893

Many tugs undoubtedly had a quick, wet motion, and often must have made the lot of a photographer seem a sore trial indeed, but it seems unlikely that they could surpass the long, lean, and heavily-sparred steam yachts for really sickening oscillation, especially when sea conditions corresponded to their period of roll. Francis Herreshoff reported that the *Narada,* which closely resembled the *Erl King,* rolled so deeply on one Atlantic crossing as to dip her yardarms.[116]

Stebbins photo copy 10463

The battleship *Missouri*

October 1903

A grand photograph of the *Missouri* undergoing trials off Cape Ann. Her speed on the first run over the course was below the contracted eighteen knots, and was thus a matter of concern for her Newport News builders. A warship which failed to meet her contract speed was the source of lengthy and expensive alterations and litigation. The second run was an all-out effort. According to the *Boston Evening Transcript*'s correspondent: ". . . thick volumes of smoke, broken once in a while by vivid tongues of flame, poured from the ship's funnels as she began the homeward run."

The added labor of the stokers was rewarded. The second run more than made up for the first, and she passed by a sixth of a knot. Since the trials were made with picked stokers and engineers, picked coal, and a clean bottom, it is unlikely that the *Missouri* ever went as fast again.

The *Missouri*'s tall funnels were intended to provide good natural draft for the furnaces when steaming normally; for the trials the engineers have resorted to forced draft in the stokehold. A big warship, by its basic nature, was a very dirty machine and consumed many thousands of tons of soft coal in a year of active service. Coal was to a navy what food was to an army. Coaling ship was an all-hands evolution, and a goodly proportion of the *Missouri*'s regular complement of 800 men were regularly employed handling coal and cleaning up after the coal. No doubt a battle-station in the main top of a battleship or a cruiser would make a man happy to trade jobs with a Hoosac Tunnel track-walker, just for the fresh air.

The *Missouri* in the photograph still belongs to her builders, and she is manned by a company crew. Her master has been borrowed from a coastal steamer, and her helmsman for the trials — a very crucial position — is an old quartermaster with long service steering Atlantic greyhounds. Her decks and furnishings (we are told) are begrimed with businesslike soot from her trip up the coast.

The *Missouri* was fitted with reciprocating engines of great power, and they must have produced a wondrous din and vibration during the trials. The *Transcript* writer described his glimpse into her innards:

> It meant a new suit of clothes for any guest who attempted to descend into the engineroom during the trial. Down an iron stairway, treacherous from oil which covered it, the visitor found that to go more than halfway to the real working parts of the machinery was much like starting out in a rainstorm without an umbrella, only in this instance oil, not pure water,

was the downpour. From every part of the machinery it dripped in a perfect shower, until the engineer's force of assistants looked as if they had just emerged from a dip in the ocean.

> In the furnace compartments another gang of forty-eight men labored with might and main to keep the fires fed to the limit of their capacity. Eight men in a file, each took his turn stirring up the coal to keep a clear draft. "It is not so bad for us as you think," said one of them, after it was over. "We look as if we were nearly dead to you (he was a German but might have been taken for a Negro from his appearance), "but we have cool air down there, supplied by great fans and our only danger is to be careful not to be drawn towards the fire by the suction. The flames do not leap out, but have a tendency to draw us in, which, in my case, once nearly cost me part of my face." Iced oatmeal water was served in the engineers' and stokers' departments all through the run.

Boston Evening Transcript, October 22, 1903

The *Missouri* had the bad luck to have been built near the beginning of the great battleship construction race, and within a few years was rendered quite obsolete by giant turbine-powered ships of the *Dreadnought* type.

Warship photos seem to have been good sellers for Stebbins. In the turn-of-the-century decades interest in naval affairs was a component of popular patriotism. Since the established trials course was off Cape Ann, Stebbins was ideally situated to take dramatic photographs of new ships at high speed. Occasionally he took photographs aboard warships for the Navy or the builders. There are hundreds of warship photographs still in the collection, and a number had been copyrighted — it is ironic that most of the photographs which Stebbins felt compelled to protect are of relatively less interest today.

In a letter to Miss Addison, Stebbins' second wife recalled that photographing fast naval vessels (probably Fore River — built destroyers) was a trying business for all parties, since the skippers of the chartered tugs were often reluctant to maneuver as close to the path of the charging men-of-war as Stebbins desired.

Stebbins plate 14878

The haddock schooner *Jessie Costa*

The schooner *Jessie Costa* chases the schooner *Rose Dorothea* on the final leg of the 1907 Fishermen's Race held in Massachusetts Bay. Captain Manny Costa is at the wheel, but we can only see his hat as he crouches to leeward, watching his headsails and trying to keep his schooner moving while working her to windward. It is odd that the mainsail has only one band of reef points — it looks to be a new sail, and maybe Manny took it from the sailmakers before it was finished in order to have it stretched in time for the race. In any event, it looks as though it will have to be returned to the loft for recutting, for it has now stretched to the limit, and the "clapper" in the boom jaws is barely clear of the mast saddle, even though the throat halyard is "two blocks." The foot of a fisherman's mainsail had to be cut in conformity with the spring of the long boom, which was stayed by a lift rigged to the very end.

The *Costa* and the *Dorothea* were both fresh haddockers. Speed was an important part of the business, for a trip of fish which was suspected of being a little ripe was sent off to be smoked, and brought a much lower price. In general, the haddockers liked to be back in to T Wharf within six days of landing their first fish.[117] What with fishing all day, dressing fish, and baiting trawls half the night, the haddock fisherman got little sleep while on the grounds. A "haddocker" landed an assortment of cod, hake, and other groundfish as well, but since haddock was then in great public favor the fresh trawlers made every effort to "get on" haddock bottom.

Twenty-seven schooners had been entered in the forty-mile race, and had they all arrived Stebbins might have gotten the most spectacular photographs of his career. Fishermen were little versed in racing tactics, and cared even less for the rules, and it would have been a grand confrontation. Unfortunately, a day of light winds and the appearance of mackerel offshore kept all but five entrants from actually making it to the line. Those who did participate were very disappointed that it wasn't blowing a whole gale, for fishermen had become very sensitive to their public image as relentless sail-carriers. Undaunted, the crowd aboard the *Dorothea* has managed to break her fore topmast with the ballooner in nothing more than a regular hazy afternoon southerly breeze.

All five of the competing schooners were designed by Tom McManus, who organized the race. Tom was a popular fellow, and it is possible that the skippers were making good on past favors. Three of the schooners, including the *Dorothea* and the *Costa*, hailed from Province-town, and were manned by Provincetown Portuguese, although they fished from T Wharf.

The best Fishermen's Race of all time was held in a perfect gale of wind in 1892. The schooners left Gloucester under full sail, and each refused to be the first to take anything in. As a result, they staggered around the course in spectacular fashion, half under water, and the winner was a vessel which had just arrived that morning and was ballasted with a heavy trip of fish. It was said that the only experience which could compare with having actually been there was to hear Tom McManus' vivid description, which was delivered in the most animated and colorful fashion, and, reportedly, improved with age. According to a vintage version, the schooner that Tom was aboard elected to execute a standing jibe around a mark, and submerged to within a quarter-inch of the hatchway in which Tom was clinging, fully impressed by the situation. Had it not been for that margin, he maintained, she surely would have filled since none of the fishermen would have made a move to ease her.[118]

Stebbins plate 17991

The sloop *Athene* in a breeze

1900

The Herreshoff sloop *Athene,* her topmast housed, thrashes towards a racing mark on a breezy day off Marblehead. The wind had turned the Puritan Cup race into a duel between the *Athene* and the big schooner *Constellation.* On the windward legs the *Athene* took the lead, soaking up to weather in superior fashion; off the wind the *Constellation* took over, charging by like a train of cars. The race was twice around the course, so there was fun for all. The outcome was finally decided when the *Constellation*'s peak halyard parted, and she finished under a main trysail.

Just before she crossed the line (perhaps this is the moment) the *Athene* was caught by a "green puff" while paying off, and knocked nearly flat. William Gay, her owner, wrote many years later:

> We were told afterwards that *Athene* was a wonderful sight when we got that knockdown, and I guess she was. "Windy" Watson came alongside after the race and congratulated us warmly, saying we had sailed a fine race. It was very nice of him, and showed fine sportsmanship. One or two pictures of the *Athene* by Stebbins in that race still hang in the EYC [Eastern Yacht Club] at the head of the stairs.[119]

"Windy" Watson, otherwise known as "Nate," was the *Constellation*'s well-known sailing master. The *Constellation* does not appear in the photograph; the white schooner in the distance is probably the *Hildegarde.*

The *Athene* was seventy feet on the waterline, and one hundred two feet overall. She was a centerboarder, and drew eleven feet. In some respects she was a predecessor of the famous one-design "New York seventies" produced by Herreshoff in 1900, the year after the *Athene* was built. The "seventies" were keel yachts, and drew fifteen feet. When Mr. Gay asked Nat Herreshoff whether the *Athene* would be competitive with the new boats he was assured, "Yes, where there is less than fifteen feet of water."[120]

Stebbins copy negative 11411

The schooner yacht *Endymion*

August 1902

The schooner *Endymion*, on the New York cruise, runs past West Chop before a beautiful southwester. Right at the moment the breeze is probably going unappreciated aboard the yacht, as the tack of the main topmast ballooner has somehow gotten free, and is senselessly avoiding recapture. The shadow on the seemingly-translucent balloon jib topsail shows that the foretopsail is hurriedly being clewed up, fisherman style, preparatory to jibing the foresail across. Then, when she can be run off a bit more, with the wind just flirting around the end of the main boom, the ballooner will probably give up its game.

Before synthetics, light sails were cut from very lovely and very delicate cotton cloth, and many were lost over an active racing season. In 1905 the owner of a big schooner estimated his annual sailmakers' bill at $6500.[121]

Looking up hazy Vineyard Sound we can see much of the fleet far astern, against the Elizabeth Islands. The run from Brenton Reef to the Vineyard was long enough to give the bigger schooners a chance to run away from the common pack if they got their wind, and was a famous part of the cruise. Once, as the schooner *Queen Mab* went barreling through the smaller fry, a New York "fifty" cleverly got on her quarter wave and was "towed" along by her, thereby winning the Astor Cup in the sloop class.[122]

The schooners of this period were intended primarily for cruising, and accordingly did not suffer from rule-cheating. The *Endymion* was only young Clinton Crane's second major design, but he did well. Although she had a clipper bow, her forefoot was cut away in modern fashion, and her keel had great drag. She was said to steer very well when running before big seas. In 1900 she set an Atlantic record of thirteen days, eight hours, New York to the Isle of Wight. This was eclipsed several years later by Charlie Barr with the schooner *Atlantic*.

Crane described the *Endymion*'s shakedown cruise:

Endymion was completed in December, 1899, and George Day [her owner] told me that he was very anxious to make the record run from New York to Bermuda. My suggestion was . . . to wait inside the Hook for a northwest gale.

Day had a seagoing skipper named Loesch, who was quite game to make the experiment. So early in February of 1900, when the weather report predicted a gale, we repaired to Sandy Hook and got under way a little before noon under four lower sails. It was beginning to blow very hard, and before dark Captain Loesch decided to take in the mainsail. Then we set a squaresail and took in the foresail. About nine o'clock that night the squaresail blew out of the boltropes. I can see it now, sailing ahead of us in the starlight and disappearing in the distance. Before we could get in jib and staysail, the jib had flapped itself apart, and for two days and two nights *Endymion* sailed before the wind under bare poles.

All the old sea dogs had told me that a long counter was unfit to go to sea. I disagreed with the old sea dogs, and gave *Endymion* a long overhang aft, as I felt it would tend to keep the breaking seas from coming on board. As I was curious to see whether I was right, I lay on the extreme afterdeck watching the combers come from astern and break. Invariably, before the white water could reach the stern, up it would go, and the crest of the wave would come aboard about opposite the mainmast as the *Endymion* rolled . . . About eleven o'clock [one] night, when I was lying on my bunk suffering severely from the pangs of seasickness, I heard a commotion in the pantry and the Captain's voice raised in anger to our steward. "Sick, are you? I'll teach you to be sick! Get in there and clean up that mess!" This . . . was the old-fashioned sea captain's idea of what discipline meant at sea, but, needless to say, we lost our steward in Bermuda.[123]

Stebbins copy negative 13576

The banana steamer *Brewster*

November 1908

The German banana steamer *Brewster*, under charter to United Fruit Company, departs Boston for San Antonio, Jamaica. Probably most fruit steamers were then English- or Norwegian-flag. They were generally fast little vessels, often twin-screw, and especially fitted for the trade. Since the holds were often refrigerated and must have developed much condensation, the tarps over the *Brewster*'s cargo booms may indicate that the hatches have recently been open for ventilation. The hatches were primarily intended for working general cargoes in the off-season, since the bananas were worked through the square ports in the steamer's side. The canvas ash chute used by the stokers after cleaning the fires hangs overboard amidships.

This is technically a very successful photograph for the period. Because of the photochemical properties of the emulsions then in use, it was ordinarily impossible to achieve a good balance between the physical subject and the sky. The problem was more severe with landscapes than with seascapes, and frequently resulted in loss of the cloud image. In this instance, however, the tones of sea and sky are more nearly matched, and we get a taste of the dark and rapidly moving cloud cover.

It is also a very elemental and successful photograph in spirit. The tug off to port, toward the Graves Light, is a creature of the harbor, with one leg ashore, and will soon be left astern with the receding islands and lighthouses. There is a strong sense of putting out to sea here, as we watch the *Brewster* begin to rise and fall with the first offshore swells, and we can imagine the raw northwesterly wind that is blowing across her open bridge. The bundled helmsman is probably experiencing the curious combination of relief and regret which outward-bound seamen have felt since the time of the Phoenicians. The photograph makes the water look very wet and liquid, and the land solid, reassuring, yet fast-disappearing.

Wind, water, ship, and land are the elements of a seaman's world. Land is the easiest concept to understand — you can jump on it, build a house on it, and only rarely will it swallow you up. Wind is first cousin to water, and water is the opposite of land. Most of the world is owned by water, and life on the land is regulated by water. The spirit of water cannot be contained or domesticated, and every humiliated sinkful is really on a journey back to the sea, that mystical immensity which takes no notice of tiny ships suspended over its dark depths.

In the nineteenth century there was still an intriguing sense of the unknown associated with life at sea, maintained partly at the expense of sailors and little ships which cleared ports on routine voyages and disappeared without trace. Today, science and technology are attempting to program the ancient mysteries of the sea into a system. It is reassuring to learn that the several VLC (Very Large Carrier) tankers which have recently been torn apart by spontaneous explosions while returning empty to the Persian Gulf have then permitted themselves to sink beneath the surface, and presumably reached the bottom as surely as any foundered little iron collier of the nineteenth century.

Stebbins plate 19073

The fishing sloop *Olive E.*

The Noank-type sloop *Olive E.*, of Newport, outward bound for swordfish. The striker, holding his long harpoon-pole, poses for Stebbins in the pulpit. The lily-iron on the end of the pole detaches after it has been stuck into a fish, and is connected by a line to a quarter-barrel in the cockpit. When a fish is ironed the keg is thrown over, and the fish is then played and killed from the dory, which is presently towing astern.

The swordfish season began in June and usually ended far to the eastward in the late summer. The early grounds were off Block Island and Nomans Land, but by August the best chances would be on South Shoals off Nantucket, and on Georges.[124] The *Olive E.* looks to be well-down with heavy cakes of ice, and she is no doubt headed to the eastward.

Most Noank-type sloops were smaller, plumb-stemmed, centerboard vessels. The *Olive E.* is of a larger class, and is apparently a keel model. Built in the New London customs district in 1894, she is the image of practicality. Her thirteen-foot beam provides a roomy cockpit and a stable hull for fishing. Her sail plan need be no larger, for in light air she has the use of a gasoline auxiliary installed shortly after the turn of the century. It is probably a reliable one-cylinder model with make-and-break ignition and a heavy flywheel; judging from her speed it is running now, as smoothly as a one-cylinder watch, and making its presence well known through the dry exhaust pipe on deck aft.

Two reefing pennants are kept rove-off in readiness; the third band is for when things really begin to hum. The gaskets, very sensibly, are made-up right on the boom. The headsail with the odd little club is self-tending, and bullseyes have been used wherever a block will not be missed. The vang on the gaff was no doubt a great help when lowering sail at sea, and the angle of the pulpit platform is thoughtfully intended to provide the striker with a comfortable stance for ironing fish. One — and only one — set of shrouds has been rattled down, and men spotting fish from aloft can each crook an arm around the stubby little topmast, which is no longer than it need be. There is precious little wasted motion aboard the *Olive E.*, for she is a no-nonsense little hooker.

The manifest advantages of the internal combustion engine were quickly realized by fishermen, and vessel design soon reflected the new influence. The Noank-type sloop rapidly evolved into the Stonington-type western-rigged dragger, which may still be found doing good work in southern New England waters. They are able and admirable little vessels, fully worthy of their ancestry.[125]

In the early 1900's many catboats, sloops, and schooners spent the summer pursuing swordfish, which had once been considered as undesirable as shark for eating. In some years swordfishing was a very profitable enterprise, and it involved a good deal more sport and a good deal less drudgery than other fisheries. Locating, spotting, and harpooning swordfish entailed skill, knowledge, and the thrill of hunting. Playing a swordfish from a dory was much more fun than baiting up endless trawls, or slaving away at the oar of a seineboat. An average swordfish weighs more than three hundred pounds and is heavily armed and dangerous. Occasionally an angry fish would attack a dory, usually with some success, and at such moments a doryman found his profession as exciting and dangerous as he could wish.

Unfortunately, this is quite a rare photo. The only other Stebbins photographs which depict fishermen actually fishing are several views showing menhaden purse seiners in Boston Harbor.

Stebbins plate 17233

The fishing schooner *Ellen C. Burke*

A fine photograph of the newly-built Boston dory trawler *Ellen C. Burke*. Around 1900 a number of big schooners were built for haddock fishing out of Boston, and the Stebbins Collection includes portraits of several. The *Burke* has hoisted her jib topsail, called the "ballooner"; the four-cornered "fisherman staysail," which sets between the masts, is presently collapsed beneath the foresail, but will soon follow. The "fisherman" was not carried when beating out of a narrow channel, as it had to be doused whenever the schooner was tacked. The two men standing beyond the anchor stock are adjusting something on the bridle of the vestigial "skull-cracker" club of the "jumbo," or forestaysail.

The *Burke* is a fine example of the deep "round-stemmed" schooners designed by Tom McManus. Like most members of the Boston and Gloucester fleet, she was built at Essex. McManus was the first to introduce the cutaway forefoot to the fishing fleet, and these schooners were said to be the first which could lay to under a foresail. With the foresheet somewhat slacked, and the helm down and in a becket, the schooners would alternately bear up and fall off, slowly drawing to windward.[126]

The schooners of this period represented a considerable advance over the old, shoal, clipper type which had dominated the New England fisheries for many years. Much of the credit for the improvement in hull form, beginning in the eighties, belongs to Boston designers, including Edward Burgess, D. J. Lawlor, Arthur Binney, and B. B. Crowninshield, who were as well or better known for their yacht work. McManus was an exception in that his immediate background was as a fish dealer, but he was friendly with the trained and established designers and was familiar with their thinking. The fresh fishery, in particular, required powerful models which could be hard-driven, and it is said that some of the designers may have complied too well, producing overly-stiff vessels which were wasteful of spars. Accordingly, McManus schooners from about 1902 onward were apparently somewhat less stiff.[127]

Probably the greatest positive effect of yachting on the improvement of fisherman design was simply the fact that the lucrative yachting market allowed for the training and maintenance of talented designers who otherwise would have had to seek different careers.

Although the educated "brain men" were able to influence the shape of schooner hulls, they were apparently unable to make many changes in sail plan, rigging, or furniture. While an ill-at-ease fishing skipper might have been duly intimidated by arcane explanations of "wave-line-wave-form" theories, no one was about to instruct him in the manner of rigging his schooner. According to Professor George Owen:

> It is interesting to note that, although these fast and able fishing schooners were of beautiful models, of sturdy construction and were vitally dependent on the strength and efficiency of sails and rigging, apparently none of the engineering lessons taught by the intensive racing of large yachts of that period was applied to those schooners. The latest built fishing schooners used the same type of rig with the same crude details as nearly a century before. The fact that the owners and crews of these vessels stuck to the schooner rig — considered by many experts as the worst of all seagoing rigs — is a tribute to their courage and hardihood.[128]

These remarks were addressed at a gathering of naval architects, where they undoubtedly received a more favorable reception than they would have before a group of retired T Wharf skippers. An "expert's" chief complaint would probably have concerned the huge, dangerous mainsail, which he most likely would have preferred moved forward, as in a ketch rig. The fishermen, of course, would have considered this an outright act of castration. They even resisted well-meaning attempts to rig the main booms with double lifts and lazy-jacks, claiming that this arrangement might interefere with the descent of a sail dropped on the run. Only the large crews of fishermen made carrying these mainsails tenable.

Stebbins plate 13970

The *Ellen C. Burke*'s narrow, tucked-up stern and pronounced sheer were typically McManus, and represented the turnabout from the old clipper model afterbody, which was characterized by a long shoal run and wide heavy quarters. Trawlers were built low-waisted to facilitate the handling of dories, gear, and fish. Trawl tubs line the cabin top, which is a comfortable height for the fishermen to stand to and bait up. The heavy plank the tubs rest on served as a bait-cutting board.

A trawl, basically, was a very long line, often over a mile in length, armed with a baited hook (fastened by a short "ganging" line) every six feet of its length. The baited trawl was set along the bottom and was worked from a dory. Most Boston haddock schooners fished ten "double-banked" (two man) dories. Dory trawling on Georges was particularly difficult on account of the strong tides.

Haddock schooners rarely anchored on the grounds, but jogged to leeward of the dories during the day. Shooting a big schooner safely alongside a loaded dory required great skill. Many dorymen were lost when, in a rising wind or squall, the three men customarily left in charge of the suddenly-overpowered schooner were unable to keep the vessel off. As a precaution, the mainsails were usually kept reefed while on the grounds in winter, and frequently chafed through at the reef points before being otherwise worn out.[129]

Tom McManus designed nearly five hundred fishing vessels in his career. He is credited with designing the first knockabout fishing schooners, which had no bowsprits and less overhang to the main boom, and were inspired by the small yacht classes of similar concept. The knockabouts were intended to end the nuisance of locked horns around T Wharf, and to preserve the lives of fishermen. Most men who were lost from bowsprits were probably simply washed off by the steep seas on the fishing banks, although an appreciable number were evidently victims of rotten sail stops and footropes.[130] Odd as it may seem, the lack of proper care of such vital gear was most likely a reflection of the average fisherman's casual approach towards his own safety, and his stubborn refusal — especially when fishing on a vessel hailing from a major port — to do maintenance, which, according to the fisheries' precise system of duties and obligations, was the owner's responsibility.

B. B. Crowninshield was another Boston designer who appears to have been both amused and intrigued by his fishermen clients, who, no doubt, were quite a contrast to his usual yachtsmen customers. In February 1906 he made a trip to Georges aboard the haddocker *Tartar*, an eighty-ton schooner of his design.

. . . we were gone just eight days and returned with sixty thousand haddock, which sold at T Wharf for exactly three-fourths cent a pound, which just paid expenses. On this trip, after fishing for six days the wind shifted to the northwest and Captain Tom Sommers decided to go home: we had been jogging around most of this time under reefed mainsail, foresail, and jumbo; for two days it blew so hard that we could not fish at all. We had neither chronometer nor sextant, only a compass and a lead which was always well primed with tallow and frequently hove; also, of course, a good chart of Gorges Shoal. I asked the skipper if he knew where we were, to which he replied that he knew exactly and promised that the next afternoon at three o'clock we would pick up Highland Light; and sure enough we did, and at eight-thirty we tied up at T Wharf.[131]

Stebbins plate 13970 (detail)

The coal schooner *Mertie B. Crowley*

The six-masted schooner *Mertie B. Crowley*, of Boston, bound south from Boston for a Middle Atlantic or Hampton Roads coal port. The big schooners had the vital ability to sail empty, without ballast. When light, they exposed a great area of windage and made plenty of leeway, creating roiled swirls along the windward waterline. (At least one Maine mariner called the swirls "pawdawgers" after the shipyard pod augers they resembled.)[132] After five thousand or so tons of bituminous are poured into the *Crowley* at the coal wharf her waterline will be even with the top of her rudder.

The *Crowley* is shown new, still fitted with all five of her topmast staysails, which are set in addition to her regular gaff topsails. The low-lying land ahead appears to be Race Point at the tip of Cape Cod, and even if the tide is running very hard indeed, the *Crowley* will probably have to tack to get by. Then, all the topsails except the spanker topsail will have to be clewed up and then reset. It is possible that her tug (with Stebbins aboard) has been sent along on the chance that it can give her a timely lift to windward; otherwise the *Crowley* may be quite a while working out of Massachusetts Bay, especially if she loses the tide while tacking for searoom.

Sail handling aboard a big schooner involved less actual "pully-haully" than aboard a smaller "hand puller," since all of the big schooners were fitted with steam winches for working sail, pumping out, and getting anchors. (Coastwise navigation involved frequent anchoring.) Nevertheless, given the great size of the gear and the small size of the crews, sail handling aboard a big schooner was anything but easy or monotonous.

The photograph gives a vivid impression of the heavy, overhanging quarters, which were unsupported when the vessel was light. Wooden construction was very supple, and the ends worked in opposition to the buoyant mid-body, causing the schooners to hog. When loaded, the hulls were subjected to severe strains from the opposite direction. As a result, all the schooners leaked to some degree. (Another photograph shows what appears to be the *Crowley*'s yawlboat — which was normally carried on the stern davits — on deck forward, presumably for repairs.)

The launching dates of the more than three hundred Eastern four-masted schooners built before 1910 stretch over a thirty-year period, peaking in 1890. By contrast, forty-three of the forty-five five-masters built before 1910, and all ten of the six-masters, were launched within a ten-year period ending in 1909. Construction of the five- and six-masters resulted in large part from a lack of organization in the booming bituminous coal business, which subjected colliers to frequent loading delays. Steam colliers were unprofitable under such circumstances, and did not enter the trade until about 1910, when conditions improved. The schooners did meet strong competition from barge lines, however.[133]

A great schooner operating coastwise was one of the most exacting commands in all of seafaring. Given the countless difficulties met while sailing a big schooner on soundings in crowded waters, along a dangerous coast, with no electronics, the average twelve years of vessel life was an impressive achievement.[134]

The great coal schooners were the last and the largest sailing vessels built by the wooden shipbuilders of Maine. From the moment of launching a big schooner lived on borrowed time, imperiled by the hazards of the trade, structural deterioration, and economic obsolescence. It is wrong, however, to suppose that their builders and operators were blind, unrealistic traditionalists. On the contrary, they built the vessels in the shrewd expectation of realizing relatively short-term profits, and many were well rewarded.[135] They built of wood because wooden construction was cheap and available.

The Stebbins Collection contains many photos of coasting schooners. Many are of Massachusetts-managed vessels, and appear to have been taken in the course of regular business. The tantalizing glimpses of schooners in the backgrounds of yachting photos indicate that Stebbins had no particular interest in coasters, which were far too common to be considered novel. The schooner which most caught public attention was the steel seven-masted freak *Thomas W. Lawson*. One of Stebbins' photographs of the *Lawson* has possibly been the most frequently reproduced marine photograph of all time.

Fourteen of Stebbins' coasting schooner photographs are currently in print in *Portrait of a Port*; hence the decision to include but two in this selection.

Stebbins plate 18171

The sloop *Hiawatha*

1898

The keel sloop *Hiawatha*, designed and built by William Eddy of Marblehead in 1888. The cut of her sails complements her sheer, and there is an active chuckle of water at her stem.

The essence of yachting is not racing nor clubs nor power boats nor even money. It is simply the act of sailing a small boat for pleasure. A small boat, in the ideal, is a mystical meeting ground wherein peaceful and practical skills of man are interwoven with wind and water, imparting to all a new and better quality.

Every society has certain unique little corners of life which can never be fully experienced by people of later times. These occasions are not of great historic importance, may be largely unrelated to the prevailing social conditions, and may, in fact, have more to say about subsequent times than they do about their own. The realm of small boat sailing in the late nineteenth century was one of those special moments, providing small boat sailors with experiences of rare pleasure.

The waters were cleaner then, the days were quieter, and the shorelines were greener. Every boat was a hand-built individual, and it is easy to recall the name of a vessel which is an individual, even if the name itself is not especially memorable. But there is no future in trying to impart character to an uninteresting boat through a name, for it will not stick. This may explain why so many modern, mass-produced boats are never named, and why even the smallest olden craft all were.

This is not intended as an empty-headed lament for old designs and materials. Every new design must be an attempt to satisfy particular requirements of service within prevailing practical limitations. Wood rots and cotton rots, and there is no great charm to rot. Good wood and good carpenters are in short supply. Fiber glass and metal hulls are now generally preferable, and modern rigs are wonders of simplicity. But there remains a need for consideration of the spiritual aspects of sailing. A boat is very much an extension of her owner.

The *Hiawatha* would be a thing of beauty simply swinging from her mooring, and a twilight sail would involve more pure sensual pleasures than a season's worth of many modern craft. Her shapely hull is planked with aromatic cedar. The appearance of her tapered and varnished spruce spars on a foggy morning Down East would be a delightful addition to the subconscious memory. Her sails are of soft and sun-smelling cotton, and her mast-hoops and reef points would tap and patter gently in expectation of slipping the mooring. The image of the big gaff-headed wall of a mainsail sheeted well-out would be good to savor when one is drifting off to sleep in February. Of course, the sail must be reefed with some frequency, but that is really not such a terrible ordeal, despite the modern notion equating reefing with fighting Indians or wrestling grizzlies. The long stinger of a bowsprit would likewise now be considered a dangerous anachronism, no doubt laden with indelicate Freudian connotations. Nevertheless, it gives the *Hiawatha* a certain stance of distinction; provides a fine place from which to watch her at play; and puts some adventure into the life of every boy who is called upon to furl the jib.

Before auxiliary engines, the average small boat sailor had to be a better seaman than his modern counterpart, and he had to approach sailing with a different philosophy. While he might not enjoy being becalmed out for a damp night, he had to occasionally accept it. Vessel handling under sail in confined waters can be an eminently satisfying business.

Even when compared to the little *Hiawatha*, sailing a large modern boat is nearly foolproof, spiritually empty, and commonly boring. Aboard a vessel of molded chemicals one sits in a cockpit reminiscent of a child's plastic play-pool, looking up at a pale and skinny sail excreted by the petro-chemical industry and hung on a noisy mast devised from a length of irrigation pipe. With the coming of night, the turning of the tide, or the dropping of the breeze the engine is quickly started, ending the delicate relationship between the sailor and his boat and the real world.

Of course, boating is now more accessible than it was in 1898, and that is progress of a sort. But in 1898 the sailor was lord of all he surveyed, and did not have to endure the mindless circlings of water-skiers. The fragile little harbors he slipped into with the last breeze of twilight were not already crowded with noisy packs of cruisers, nor were the shores overbuilt with brightly-lit cottages.

For many years, there were some very enjoyable cruises, generally to the Eastward, among the thirty, forty, and forty-six footers. Oh, how delightful it was, after a hard day's scrapping, to make a quiet harbor and then visit one another's boats, and encased in a comfortable cabin with broad transoms, comfortable cushions, and all that goes in making true comfort, to sit and spin yarns . . . [136]

Stebbins plate 9378

Bibliography

Notes on the Introduction

1. Charles B. Hosmer, *Presence of the Past* (New York: Putnam, 1965), p. 263.
2. Statement of Robert Weinstein, Los Angeles, California.

Notes on the Text

3. Francis Herreshoff, *An Introduction to Yachting* (New York: Sheridan House, 1963), p. 75.
4. W. P. Stephens, *Traditions and Memories of American Yachting* (New York: Motor Boating, 1942), pp. 18–25.
5. *The Rudder, Sail and Paddle*, 3 (June 1892).
6. C. P. Kunhardt, *Small Yachts* (New York: Forest and Stream, 1891), p. 167.
7. Hyde Windlass Co. advertisement in the Bath Marine Museum Library; Frederick C. Mathews, *American Merchant Ships* (Salem: Marine Research Society, 1931), ser. ii, p. 180.
8. C. F. Adams in C. H. W. Foster, *The Eastern Yacht Club Ditty Box* (Boston, 1932), p. 114.
9. N. G. Herreshoff in Foster, *Ditty Box*, pp. 139–40.
10. George Owen, "Outstanding New England Types of Fishing Boats, Whalers and Yachts," *Historical Transactions* (New York: Society of Naval Architects and Marine Engineers, 1945), p. 155.
11. Foster, *Ditty Box*, p. 61.
12. Stephens, *Traditions*, p. 169.
13. Edward Burgess in N. L. Stebbins, *American and English Yachts* (New York: Scribner's, 1887), p. 8.
14. Capt. W. J. L. Parker, USCG Ret., "To 'The River': An Offshore Schooner Trade," a paper delivered at the Bath Marine Museum, May 1973, p. 2.
15. Ibid., pp. 6–7.
16. Ibid., pp. 7–10.
17. Ibid., p. 11.
18. *Coronet Memories* (New York, 1899), p. 220.
19. Alfred E. Loomis, *Ocean Racing* (New York: Morrow, 1938), pp. 35–53.
20. Lt. William King in Fred S. Cozzens, *The History of American Yachting* (New York: Cassell, 1888), p. 117.
21. *Coronet*, p. 219.
22. Ibid., p. 86.
23. Stephens, *Traditions*, p. 170.
24. Ibid., p. 167.
25. Hull Yacht Club yearbook, 1893.
26. *New York Times*, July 10, 1888.
27. Herreshoff, *Introduction*, p. 73.
28. Capt. R. F. Coffin in Cozzens, *History of American Yachting*, pp. 67, 69; Stephens, *Traditions*, p. 35.
29. Stephens, *Traditions*, p. 36.
30. Ibid., p. 40.
31. Herreshoff, *Introduction*, p. 95.
32. Stephens, *Traditions*, p. 85.
33. Ibid., p. 47.
34. Ibid., p. 85; Coffin in Cozzens, pp. 88, 89, 91.
35. Charles S. Morgan, *Shipbuilding on the Kennebunk* (Kennebunkport: Kennebunkport Historical Society, 1970), pp. 29–32.
36. Lt. W. J. Lewis Parker, USCG, *The Great Coal Schooners of New England 1870–1909* (Mystic: Marine Historical Association, 1948), pp. 9–27.
37. Jennie C. Everson, *Tidewater Ice of the Kennebec River* (Freeport: Bond Wheelwright, 1970).
38. Charles L. Poor, *Men Against the Rule* (New York: New York Yacht Club, 1937), pp. 28–30.
39. Coffin in Cozzens, pp. 64, 90, 98, 99.
40. Lewis Herreshoff in *Yachting; The Badmitton Library* (London, 1894), ser. ii, p. 262.
41. W. G. Gibbons, "The Marine Ram," *United States Naval Institute Proceedings*, 8 (1882): 214.
42. *Boston Globe*, February 4, 1893.
43. W. L. Clowes, "The Ram in Action and Accident," *United States Naval Institute Proceedings*, 20 (1894): 94.

44. *New York Times*, August 30, 1891.

45. Stephens, *Traditions*, p. 80; Henry Shields, *Famous Clyde Yachts* (Glasgow, 1888).

46. Statement of Andrew Nesdall, Waban, Mass.

47. J. P. Thearly, "The Ballasting of Ocean Steamers for North Atlantic Voyages," *Transactions of the Institute of Naval Architects*, 45 (1903): 119.

48. *New York Times*, April 17, 1887, and October 11, 1889.

49. F. Chadwick et al., *Ocean Steamships* (New York: Scribner's, 1891), p. 175.

50. *The Rudder*, 9 (March 1898).

51. Clinton Crane, *Clinton Crane's Yachting Memories* (New York: Van Nostrand, 1952), p. 121; *New York Times*, June 28, 1886.

52. C. F. Adams in Foster, *Ditty Box*, p. 115.

53. *New York Times*, April 30, 1892.

54. Herreshoff, *Introduction*, pp. 133, 74.

55. E. S. Jaffray in Cozzens, p. 115.

56. B. B. Crowninshield, *Fore-and-Afters* (Boston: Houghton Mifflin Co., 1940), p. 94; Stephens, *Traditions*, p. 92; Foster, *Ditty Box*, p. 140.

57. G. A. Stewart in Henry G. Peabody, *Representative American Yachts* (Boston: Heliotype, 1893), pp. 11, 14, 15.

58. *New York Times*, July 19, 1891.

59. Stephens, *Traditions*, p. 169; Crane, *Memories*; Foster, *Ditty Box*, p. 114.

60. Herreshoff, *Introduction*, p. 98; George C. Homans, "Sailing with Uncle Charley," *The Atlantic Monthly*, July, 1965.

61. Crowninshield, *Fore-and-Afters*, pp. 90–91.

62. Duke of Beaufort, *Yachting; The Badmitton Library* (Boston, 1894), ser. i, p. 9.

63. C. J. C. McAlister in Cozzens, pp. 155–6.

64. Crowninshield, *Fore-and-Afters*, p. 69.

65. *The Rudder*, 9 (March 1898).

66. Foster, *Ditty Box*, p. 77.

67. Stephens, *Traditions*, pp. 78, 79.

68. McAlister in Cozzens, p. 146. Order of passages altered.

69. Herreshoff in *Badmitton*, ser. i, p. 262.

70. See "*Tartar*" in Stebbins, *American and English Yachts*; Howard I. Chappelle, *American Sailing Craft* (New York: Kennedy, 1936), p. 59.

71. Foster, *Ditty Box*, pp. 121–2.

72. Crane, *Memories*, p. 170.

73. Thomas W. Lawson, *The Lawson History of the America's Cup* (Boston, 1902), p. 283.

74. Statement of the late Thomas Lampee.

75. Charles I. Lampee, "Memories of Cruises on Boston Pilot Boats of Long Ago," *Nautical Research Journal*, 10 (Spring 1959): 50–51.

76. This phrase is borrowed from the classic steamboat story by Malcome MacDuffie, "Strange Voice to Starboard" in *Yankees Under Steam* (Dublin, N.H.: Yankee, 1970), p. 67.

77. Arthur L. Johnson, "The International Line," *The American Neptune*, 33 (April 1973): 91; William L. Taylor in a book review in the Harvard *Business History Review* (Summer 1972).

78. Stephens, *Traditions*, p. 45.

79. Poor, *Rule*, p. 21.

80. Numerous references in Stephens, *Traditions*.

81. Coffin in Cozzens, pp. 43–4; Foster in *Ditty Box*, p. 64; *The Rudder*, 20 (August 1908): 83; Crane, *Memories*, pp. 28, 146.

82. Charles Clay in Cozzens, p. 184.

83. Crane, *Memories*, pp. 126–8.

84. Coffin in Cozzens, p. 34.

85. Crowninshield, *Fore-and-Afters*, pp. 77–8.

86. Ibid., pp. 87–8.

87. Winfield M. Thompson, "Cats in Massachusetts Bay," *The Rudder*, 20 (August 1908): 88–9.

88. Winfield M. Thompson, "Cats in Massachusetts Bay," *The Rudder*, 20 (July 1908): 81–92.

89. Owen, "Outstanding New England Types," p. 152.

90. David Cheever, Jr., "*Ramona* Sails Again," *Yachting*, 82 (July 1947): 68.

91. *Boston Evening Transcript*, September 11, 1897.
92. Dr. William Bergan, *Old Nantasket* (Quincy, 1968).
93. Crane, *Memories*, p. 104.
94. Ibid., pp. 100–101, 130; Lawson, *History*, p. 143.
95. Herreshoff, *Traditions*, p. 123; Crane, *Memories*, p. 106.
96. W. P. Stephens, *The Rudder* 14 (May 1903).
97. Jaffray in Cozzens, p. 236.
98. *New York Times*, September 25, 1890.
99. Jaffray in Cozzens, p. 138.
100. *New York Times*, June 11, 1905.
101. Crane, *Memories*, p. 65.
102. C. F. Adams in Foster, *Ditty Box*, p. 115.
103. W. P. Stephens in Charles Kundhart, *Supplement to Small Yachts* (New York: Forest and Stream, 1896), p. 29.
104. Poor, *Rule*, pp. 43–4.
105. Ibid., pp. 44–5.
106. Crane, *Memories*, p. 186.
107. Owen, "Outstanding New England Types," p. 157; Herreshoff, *Introduction*, pp. 150–51.
108. *The Rudder*, 14 (June 1903): 356.
109. Poor, *Rule*, pp. 58–72.
110. *Fishermen of the Atlantic* (Boston, 1909), p. 85.
111. *National Fisherman* (December 1973) p. 32C.
112. *New York Times*, August 9, 1893.
113. Crane, *Memories*, p. 187.
114. Herreshoff, *Introduction*, p. 28.
115. Ibid., p. 31; *History of American Yachts and Yachtsmen* (New York: Spirit of the Times, 1901), pp. 67–8.
116. Herreshoff, *Introduction*, p. 34.
117. Crowninshield, *Fore-and-Afters*, p. 10.
118. Foster, *Ditty Box*, p. 141.
119. Ibid., p. 171.
120. Crowninshield, *Fore-and-Afters*, p. 87.
121. *New York Times*, June 11, 1905.
122. Crane, *Memories*, p. 134.
123. Ibid., pp. 36–8.
124. George Wesley Pierce, *Goin' Fishin'* (Salem: Marine Research Society, 1934), pp. 212–15.
125. Letter from Capt. Elwell B. Thomas in *The Skipper* (January 1969).
126. Crowninshield, *Fore-and-Afters*, pp. 14–15.
127. Howard I. Chapelle, *American Fishing Schooners* (New York: Norton, 1973) p. 234.
128. Owen, "Outstanding New England Types," p. 149.
129. Crowninshield, *Fore-and-Afters*, p. 10.
130. Chapelle, *Schooners*, p. 226.
131. Crowninshield, *Fore-and-Afters*, p. 11.
132. Statement of Jim Stevens, Boothbay, Maine, in reference to his father, Jacob.
133. Parker, *Coal Schooners*, pp. 120, 95.
134. Ibid., p. 90.
135. Ibid., p. 66.
136. Foster, *Ditty Box*, p. 132.